THE OPTIMISM OF

PRE-MILLENNIALISM

by

Henry Clay Morrison

First Fruits Press
Wilmore, Kentucky
c2012

asburyseminary.edu
800.2ASBURY
204 North Lexington Avenue
Wilmore, Kentucky 40390

First Fruits
THE ACADEMIC OPEN PRESS OF ASBURY SEMINARY

ISBN: 9781621710271

The Optimism of Pre-Millennialism, by Henry Clay Morrison.
First Fruits Press, © 2012
Pentecostal Publishing Company, © 1927

Digital version at
http://place.asburyseminary.edu/firstfruitsheritagematerial/17

Morrison, H. C. (Henry Clay), 1857-1942
    The optimism of pre-millennialism / by Henry Clay Morrison.
    Wilmore, Ky. : First Fruits Press, c2012.
    147 p. ; 21 cm.
    Reprint. Previously published: Louisville, Ky. : Pentecostal Publishing
    Company, c1927.
    ISBN: 9781621710271 (pbk.)
    1. Millennium (Eschatology). I. Title.
BT890 .M78 2012

Cover design by Haley Hill

asburyseminary.edu
800.2ASBURY
204 North Lexington Avenue
Wilmore, Kentucky 40390

First Fruits
THE ACADEMIC OPEN PRESS OF ASBURY SEMINARY

THE OPTIMISM OF PRE-MILLENNIALISM

BY

H. C. MORRISON, D.D.

PENTECOSTAL PUBLISHING COMPANY
Louisville, Kentucky

DEDICATION.

This volume is lovingly dedicated to all those who are "Looking for that blessed hope, and the glorious appearing of the great God and our Saviour Jesus Christ.

"Who gave himself for us, that he might redeem us from all iniquity, and purify unto himself a peculiar people, zealous of good works." 2 Tim. 2:13, 14.

CONTENTS

PREFACE.

During His ministry on earth, our Lord Jesus plainly and repeatedly taught that He would come again, personally, into this world. After His departure this teaching was held tenaciously by His disciples, and was to them a constant source of encouragement and strength as, under severe trial and persecution, they went forth to preach the gospel.

The disciples taught, and the early Christians believed, that the Lord Jesus would return to the comfort and blessing of His people and church. John, the Beloved, declares very plainly that he will come to reign and rule over the earth a thousand years.

The Christians for some three hundred years were comforted and encouraged with "this blessed hope" that Jesus was coming back to earth again to set up a kingdom of righteousness and peace among men. Out of this faith and teaching grew the doctrine of what is called "The Millennium." The reader will understand that, as the word century means a hundred years, the word millennium means a thousand years.

There has been since these early centuries of the simple and general faith in the coming of the Lord, quite a diversity of opinion on the subject among devout Christian people; some believing with the early Christians that the coming of the Lord was imminent,that He would appear in His glory to overthrow evil, cast out Satan, and set up His kingdom in the world, when the prophetic note in the angelic song announcing the birth of Christ in Bethlehem, would be fulfilled, and there would be a reign of good will among men, and God would truly be glorified; when the prophetic note in the form of prayer which Jesus gave to His disciples, would be realized, and men would do the will of God on earth, as it is done in heaven. Christians who hold to this teaching and faith are known as "Premillennialists"; in other words, that Christ's coming will be before the setting up of His kingdom, and the full and glorious power of His gospel prevails on earth.

The other branch of Christian teachers believe that the gospel will be preached with prevailing power, that all nations shall be evangelized, and that Jesus will not come in person, until the final judgment. Those who hold to this view are called "Post-millennialists."

There has been considerable discussion between these two schools of teaching among Christian people. Post-millennialists insist that Pre-millennialists have a pessimistic outlook with reference to the future history of the race; that their teaching and attitude have a tendency to paralyze effort for the social benefit and uplift of society and world evangelization.

Pre-millennialists claim that their Postmillennial brethren set up programs for the uplift and benefit of society quite apart from, and in antagonism with, the program of Christ; that they would destroy the "blessed hope" in the hearts of the disciples of our Lord, and fail to keep their lamps trimmed and burning, and that they are in danger of becoming more interested in the building up of vast human ecclesiasticisms than in vital evangelism for the rapid spread of the gospel, until all men, everywhere, shall hear the good news of salvation by faith in Christ, and His second glorious appearing.

This volume is written to show that Premillennialists are the most optimistic people in the world; that they have the brightest and most hopeful outlook for the future history of the human race. In the discussion that has been going forward between Post-

and Pre-millennialists, the Pre-millennialists have this very decided advantage: They rest their faith and arguments upon a firm foundation of many scriptures found in both the Old and New Testaments; while the Post-millennialists build their superstructure upon the sandy foundation of men's opinions without any "Thus saith the Lord" for proof of their position.

H. C. MORRISON.

THE OPTIMISM OF PRE-MILLEN-NIALISM.

CHAPTER I.

THE OPTIMISTIC OUTLOOK.

There can be no more optimistic views with regard to the final future of this world and its inhabitants, than those held by Premillennialists. They firmly believe all of those splendid prophecies contained in the Old Testament Scriptures, and those promises contained in the New Testament, concerning the coming Kingdom and reign of our Lord Jesus Christ, when "The meek shall inherit the earth," and all kingdoms shall become the kingdom of our Lord Christ, and "The earth shall be filled with the knowledge of the glory of the Lord, as the waters cover the sea."

Pre-millennialists believe that at some time in the not so distant future, the prayer that our Lord Jesus taught His followers to offer to the Father, "Thy kingdom come; thy will be done on earth, as the angels do it in heaven," will be answered. Pre-millennialists have no sympathy with the pessimistic and gloomy views of Post-millen-

9

nialists who seem to ignore the teachings of the prophets, Christ and the apostles, concerning the second coming of our Lord to inaugurate a reign of peace and good will on earth, when men shall learn war no more.

Pre-millennialists are not in harmony with the teaching and program marked out by Post-millennial adherents that, for untold thousands of years to come, the earth will be cursed with wars and bloodshed, plagues and famine, droughts and floods, and all of those disasters and sorrows which have characterized the past history of the race, and exist in the world at the present time.

The teaching of Post-millennialists that the gospel will be preached until all nations and peoples shall be saved, and that Jesus will not come until His Kingdom is set up on earth, is entirely out of harmony, and in contradiction of the plain teachings of our Lord, who assures us that, when He comes, the world will be unprepared, and many will not be in a state of salvation. He tells us, "Then shall two be in the field; the one shall be taken, and the other left. Two women shall be grinding at the mill; the one shall be taken, and the other left." Matt. 24:40, 41.

In all of Christ's teachings on this important subject, He seeks to impress upon us the fact that, many people will reject the gospel, will be unsaved, will disregard His sayings with reference to His second coming, and will be engaged in their sins and forgetfulness of God as they were when the world was destroyed by water. In the gospel of Matthew he says: "But as the days of Noe were, so shall the coming of the Son of man be. For as the days that were before the flood they were eating and drinking, marrying and giving in marriage, until the day that Noe entered into the ark, and knew not until the flood came, and took them all away; so shall also the coming of the Son of man be." Matt. 24:37, 38, 39.

There cannot be found one word in the sayings of Jesus to indicate that the whole world of mankind will have been converted, that peace will reign throughout the earth, and that in any sense His kingdom will be set up before His coming. All of His sayings are exactly the opposite to this. Read in Luke 21, verses 25, 26, 27; 34, 35, 36. "And there shall be signs in the sun, and in the moon, and in the stars; and upon the earth distress of nations, with perplexity; the sea and the waves roaring; men's hearts failing them for fear, and for looking after those things which are coming on the earth:

for the powers of heaven shall be shaken. And then shall they see the Son of man coming in a cloud with power and great glory." This is followed by a special exhortation to His disciples of all time: "And take heed to yourselves, lest at any time your hearts be overcharged with surfeiting, and drunkenness, and cares of this life, and so that day come upon you unawares. For as a snare shall it come on all them that dwell on the face of the whole earth. Watch ye therefore, and pray always, that ye may be accounted worthy to escape all these things that shall come to pass, and to stand before the Son of man.

Because Pre-millennialists believe these very clear and oft-repeated teachings of our Lord with reference to conditions when He shall come to receive His bride, and reign over His redeemed people, they are constantly accused of being pessimistic. The truth is, they simply recognize Jesus as supreme authority, take His words for their full value, look back over past history, look around them at existing conditions, and accept, without question or doubt, the teachings of the prophets, Christ and the apostles with reference to the end of this age, the coming and setting up of the kingdom of Christ.

Conditions during the World War were perhaps worse than anything described or anticipated by the most gloomy outlook of Pre-millennialists. The bloodshed, the savagery, the rape and destruction, the fiendish slaughter of untold millions of human beings, the pestilence which followed, and the famine sweeping away countless millions of mankind, exceeds anything anticipated by those who believe the teachings of the apostle who assures us that, "In the last days," that is, as we approach the end of this dispensation, "perilous times shall come."

Post-millennialism, in its unscriptural teaching with reference to the coming kingdom of Christ on earth, makes no provision for any change in physical conditions which now exist. Even after the kingdom of Christ is set up in the world, according to their views, we shall still have the wreck of earthquakes, the eruption of volcanoes, destroying their multitudes, tidal waves sweeping away the helpless people, floods, droughts, plagues and famine. No amount of intellectual development or moral uplift of society can have any effect upon these natural disturbances which have always imperiled and destroyed untold millions of human lives, and swept away the accumulated property of centuries of patient and economical toil.

Pre-millennialists believe that the coming of Jesus, the setting up of His kingdom, and the inauguration of His reign on earth, will bring in a new order of things; not only will the nations live in peace, but nature herself, which has been disturbed and thrown out of order by the prince of the power of the air, will be regulated, and the fearful catastrophes that have wasted the lives and the products of the toil of the people, will have passed away, and the desert will blossom like the rose, and there will not only be peace among men, but peace in the whole realm of the physical elements, and that Satan, with all of his diabolical powers, will be cast off the earth, and the reign of Christ will bring order and harmony, not only among men, but into the whole of the forces of nature, including the animal kingdom.

This optimistic view of the future held and insisted upon by Pre-millennialists is fully justified by such scriptures as the following: "And there shall come forth a rod out of the stem of Jesse, and a Branch shall grow out of his root: and the Spirit of the Lord shall rest upon him, the spirit of wisdom and understanding, the spirit of counsel and might, the spirit of knowledge and the fear of the Lord; and shall make him of quick understanding in the fear of the Lord: and he shall not judge after the sight of his eyes, neither reprove after the hearing of his ears: but with righteousness shall he judge the poor, and reprove with equity for the meek of the earth: and he shall smite the earth with the rod of his mouth, and with the breath of his lips shall he slay the wicked. And righteousness shall be the girdle of his loins, and faithfulness the girdle of his reins. The wolf also shall dwell with the lamb, and the leopard shall lie down with the kid; and the calf and the young lion and the fatling together; and a little child shall lead them. And the cow and the bear shall feed; their young ones shall lie down together; and the lion shall eat straw like the ox. And the sucking child shall play on the hole of the asp, and the weaned child shall put his hand on the cockatrice' den. And they shall not hurt nor destroy in all my holy mountain: for the earth shall be full of the knowledge of the Lord, as the waters cover the sea. And in that day there shall be a root of Jesse, which shall stand for an ensign of the people; to it shall the Gentiles seek: and his rest shall be glorious." Isa. 11:1-10.

The reader will readily understand that the prophet here is referring to Jesus Christ and his reign among men. There is no possible way to give an intelligent interpretation to this prophecy apart from our Lord Jesus, and His dominion and reign over men, and the bringing of peace and harmony into our world that has been cursed with strife and war among men and in the animal kingdom as well.

Studying prophecies of this character, and the teachings of our Lord Jesus and His holy apostles, Pre-millennialists are compelled to refuse to accept the gloomy and pessimistic views of the Post-millennialists, who would compel us to expect an indefinite period of time of human suffering, sorrow, war and destruction, without any reasonable hope of trimming our lamps to watch with joy for the appearing of our Redeemer and King, who came the first time in great humiliation to redeem us from our sins in His death agonies on the cross, and will come the second time in great glory to reign in peace over His redeemed people.

The optimism of Pre-millennialists is today on the tip-toe of hopefulness for the future of the world, and is breaking forth everywhere in songs of triumph and joy at the glad thought that the coming of our Lord draweth nigh, when wars shall be ended, pitiless cyclones shall no longer sweep the earth with destruction, pestilence and famine shall cease, social conditions shall be properly adjusted; the savage wild beasts shall become docile and live at peace with each other, God shall be glorified, and good will shall prevail among men, and God shall have overturned, overturned, overturned, until He has come whose right it is to reign.

CHAPTER II.

The universe did not come into existence by accident, and it is not governed by chance. "In the beginning God created." About us everywhere, we find infallible proofs of the existence and work of an intelligent Being of omnipotent power and infinite wisdom. "Day unto day uttereth speech, and night unto night sheweth knowledge."

We are surrounded with the evidences that this planet was created and furnished for the habitation of the human race. There seems to be no possible way to account for this department of our Father's great house, but that He built it, arranged it, and furnished it, to be the dwelling place of mankind. The creation of man, an immortal free being, with power to reproduce beings like himself, involves such vast possibilities of rebellion, sin and suffering, that God never would have created him if there had not been for him a place in the universe that must remain forever vacant, without his creation.

The nature of God called for such a creature. There was in the eternal Fatherhood a love that yearned for a family of beings of the nature of man, in which to invest and reveal His infinite love. Long before the first stone was laid in the superstructure God built for man's habitation, He had a fixed purpose, a definite objective in view. Looking into the endless future, contemplating His final objective, God saw the end was so great and so glorious, that He was fully justified in the whole enterprise of man's creation, with all that it involved.

When the final end is secured, when the triumphant glory is brought in, when we no longer see through a glass darkly, but face to face; when the weaving is completed, and the tapestry of human history is cut from the loom of time and shaken out in all its beauty, harmony, profound significance, and eternal glory, then we shall understand something of the divine objective, and give glory to God, who has worked so patiently throughout the ages, as He led forward the slow and stumbling feet of humanity, to the attainment of His fixed and eternal objective.

God has a fixed purpose. He saw the end from the beginning. He has met with stubborn opposition; He has had to deal with dense ignorance, but He will never make an assignment, He will never go into bankruptcy. His investments in mankind are so large, His resources are so inexhaustible, His foundations are so securely laid, His love is so infinite, in the gift of His Son He has paid so large a price for the redemption of the race that He cannot fail. Jesus shall reign until all of His enemies are placed beneath His feet, and the culmination of God's great objective shall be so complete, so eternal, and so glorious, that Jesus "shall see the travail of his soul, and shall be satisfied."

The teachings of the Apostle John in his Epistle to the Ephesians shall be fully realized: "According as he hath chosen us in him before the foundation of the world, that we should be holy and without blame before him in love." Read also the tenth and eleventh verses: "That in the dispensation of the fulness of times he might gather together in one all things in Christ, both which are in heaven, and which are on earth; even in him. In whom also we have obtained an inheritance, being predestinated according to the purpose of him who worketh all things after the counsel of his own will." Eph. 1:4, 10, 11.

In the fifth chapter of Revelation we catch a glimpse of the final glory which shall come out of the whole enterprise of the creation of man, and the difficulties God has had to contend with in bringing about the fulness of His great objective. Let us read of this final glory in verses 11, 12 and 13: "And I beheld, and I heard the voice of many angels round about the throne and the beasts and the elders: and the number of them was ten thousand times ten thousand, and thousands of thousands; Saying with a loud voice, Worthy is the Lamb that was slain to receive power, and riches, and wisdom, and strength, and honor, and glory, and blessing. And every creature which is in heaven, and on the earth, and under the earth, and such as are in the sea, and all that are in them, heard I saying, Blessing, and honor, and glory, and power, be unto him that sitteth upon the throne, and unto the Lamb for ever and ever."

With this fixed objective, looking forward to these glorious results, God built this globe for our habitation, peopled it with an intelligent race of immortal beings, placed us on probation, when we sinned, gave His Son for our redemption, fixed a period for the spread of the gospel, through which we are now passing, and which, in harmony with the teachings of the Holy Scriptures, is now approaching an end and the inauguration of the kingdom of God on earth, which shall go forward in its blessedness for a number of centuries, and shall finally come to the day of judgment and the ushering in of the glorious conditions described in the quotation above from the Book of Revelation.

We do not believe that a God of infinite wisdom and love would have created the race at all, if He had not been able to look forward to a time of a reign of peace, a warless world, a race redeemed. He has moved slowly toward His grand objective because man is so crippled by sin, so slow to understand, that he cannot move rapidly, and God has cut down His strides in order to accommodate them to man's poor capacity to go forward with Him. There has never been a time in the long, weary progress of the race, in the ebb and flow of good and evil, in the grief and sorrow over the wickednes of mankind, when God has said to the angels, "I do not know what to do next." He always knows what to do next, and every movement in the vast scheme of creation and redemption on the part of God, is a forward movement.

It must be remembered that man is an intelligent, free being. He cannot be compelled to be good. The divine method is not one of compulsion; in the nature of things, it cannot be. It is a method of revelation, reasoning, persuasion, and appeal to man to make his own choice. The veil of the future is lifted; man is taught that physical life upon this globe is of short duration and uncertain, but that he is an immortal being, that eternal years await him in a future state, that his conduct and character here fix his destiny there. When man sinned he was taught that mercy provided a way of salvation. From the lips of Jesus he learned that God, like a compassionate father, awaits the coming home of the prodigal with open arms, with every provision for his complete restoration, communion and fellowship with his Father. Let us repeat what we have hitherto said in this chapter: the nature of God called for such a being as man, one with whom He could commune, in whom He could invest His love and lift up into eternal harmony and rulership with Himself. Man is greater than we have realized. God estimates him much higher than he estimates himself. Jesus teaches us that he would make a bad bargain if he exchanged his soul for the whole world.

Think of a father dwelling in a mansion, with millions at his command, and no children upon whom to bestow his riches; an affectionate father longing for companionship from those near and dear, upon whom he could lavish his affections. Think of a Shakespeare with his brain full of moving pictures and tremendous tragedies, and no pen, paper, or amanuensis with which to express his thought; of a Milton with his vast flights of imagination, and no possibility of imparting to others the scenes which he beheld. Think of Michael Angelo, with his wonderful paintings in his brain; they sweep in a panorama of beauty before his vision, but he has no canvas, no brush, no paint with which to make his dreams come true, and his heavenly visions to stand out, enchanting the millions who have stood uncovered before his masterpieces. Try to conceive of a God, the Creater of this vast universe, and so full of love that He would give His own Son to die for the redemption of the most sinful and degraded and yet, no intelligent, reciprocating human being to love. This could not be. The infinite Father must have a family, even if some of His children will go astray, trample upon His commandments, reject his mercies, and grieve His love. Hence, man's existence, and the plans stretching through the ages, ever leading forward to the consummation of an objective so vast and eternal that it sweeps entirely beyond the possibility of our comprehension, but no doubt, will give us delightful entertainment, developing study and glorious discovery through the eternal years. God's eternal objective justifies the adventure of the creation of intelligent, moral beings, and the investment of all that had gone into the plan of human redemption, and the weary centuries of forward movement to the final consummation of His objective.

CHAPTER III.

THE DIVINE PROGRAM.

The architect of a great building looks upon the completed structure with his mind's eye before the laying down of the first stone for the foundation. He knows what the building will be in all of its proportions and the uses to which it will be devoted, before drawing plans and specifications for its construction. This is eminently true of the great Architect of the universe. God knew exactly what He proposed to do before He drew His plans. The specifications are on a scale much larger than our capacity for comprehension, but God, from the beginning, knew what His purpose was and what His plans must be in order to the consummation of His infinite purpose.

There is divine order throughout the universe; there is constant forward movement toward the great objective. God has a program and things take place in this world in harmony with His pre-arranged plans, looking to the fulfillment and consummation of His eternal purpose. We have no reference here to fatalism, but we are thinking of an intelligent, divine order.

The Holy Scriptures reveal the fact,

which is corroborated by human history,
that God has broken up time into dispensations, or ages. It is easy for us to mark off
three distinct dispensations: The dispensation of the Father, the dispensation of the
Son, and the dispensation of the Holy Ghost,
all combining and moving forward toward
the setting up of the kingdom of God on
earth.

In addition to these dispensations it
seems God has marked off certain periods,
or epochs, in human history. The first division of history began with the creation of
Adam and closed with the flood. Man had
become desperately wicked; he refused to
hear the warnings of God's prophet, hard-
ened his heart, and plunged into deeper
depths of sin. There is an inevitable law in
the divine government that those who will
not give heed to warning, who trample upon
divine commandments, refuse divine mercy,
and will not repent, must suffer divine judgment. Those who will not surrender and
seek salvation must inevitably perish. God
always gives warning to men and nations.
Judgment, in the nature of things, must follow rejected mercy. God can no more be indifferent to the moral law which governs
men, than He can be indifferent to the physical laws which govern the planets.

In His wisdom God has appointed that there should be a winter season for the rest and refreshing of the earth, for the decay of vegetation to fertilize the soil; a time when trees and growing things should thrust their roots downward deep into the earth and gather strength for the bearing of the larger vegetation and increased growth of the coming summer. He appointed springtime for planting, the summer for growth, and the autumn for the ripening and gathering in of the harvest.

God directs the course of the clouds wafted upon the wind bearing the waters which have been gathered from lakes and ocean, bringing refreshing rains to mountains and plains to keep the springs bursting forth with drink, to water the growing harvests, to send the rills singing on their way, and the rivers to cool the summer's heat, and bear man's commerce upon their bosoms. There is a wonderful and beautiful order in God's creation. Life upon the planet would become impossible if God should break up this order; if all the rain should fall in the winter season, if drought should blast the crops in the springtime, and heavy snows should fall, breaking down and rotting the ripening crops in August.

There must be order in the moral world.

There are certain fundamental laws enacted by divine wisdom that must be enforced if civilization is preserved, if progress is to be made in scientific discovery, and the varied and abundant resources with which God has supplied us are to be utilized and enjoyed by the race. In order to a progressive civilization, there must be the protection and preservation of the purity of the family, the integrity of the civil government, the proper adjustment of social conditions, and the spirituality of the Church. There are no whims or tyrannies in the moral laws of God; they are absolutely necessary; they are legislated for man's protection, his happiness here and eternal welfare hereafter.

God cannot permit His moral laws to be ignored or violated. No intelligent governor can look with indifference upon the violation of the laws of the state over which he presides; no just judge can permit criminals to go unpunished from his court. The moral world would inevitably go into wreck and ruin if God gave no laws for its regulation, or failed to enforce those laws and inflict the penalties attached when those laws are violated. There come times in the history of an individual, a community, or a nation, or the entire world, when laws have been violated, mercy has been rejected, and

God issues a warrant for the arrest and punishment of the individual or the people who ruthlessly trample upon divine law and bring disorder and chaos into the moral world.

The antediluvians had reached the limit of wickedness; they refused to repent. God must give up the whole purpose for an inspired Book, the coming of His Son, of the organization of His Church, the spread of the gospel, and the final setting up of His kingdom on earth, or He must gather out the few faithful souls and sweep away the rebellious and impenitent wicked, with a flood.

It was for this very reason that God broke up human history into dispensations —ages and epochs. He knew that men would become wicked and rebellious; they would refuse to listen to reason; they would trample upon His commandments and spurn His mercy. He knew that they would bring about moral conditions that would hinder progress and blight the race; and He was compelled to fix certain bounds, to appoint times of reckoning, and now and then, to bring in a day of judgment; not the final judgment at the end of the ages, but the closing up of the work of an age, the balancing of the books, the selecting of the wheat

from the chaff, the plowing under of the
refuse, debris and waste of time, and the
sowing of the good wheat, the pure and holy
characters, gathered out of the harvest, to
produce a larger and better crop for moral
progress and spiritual development.

It is thus that the program of God moves
forward; it is thus that with infinite patience He labors with sinful humanity, judg
ments never coming until mercy is ex-
hausted; but finally, the messenger calling
to repentance, and offering pardon and
peace, is recalled, and the angel of judgment, with a drawn sword, goes forth. Woe
be to the individual, the community, or the
nation when destruction becomes necessary,
when it is a mercy to the future of the race
to remove out of the way a people who
would thwart the plan of God, who would
break up and destroy moral government,
who would quench and put out all spiritual
fires which illuminate the pathway of the
race moving forward in fulfillment of the
eternal plans of our Creator. Judgments of
destruction never come until it is absolutely
necessary that they should come in order to
preserve the moral integrity of God's government and bring the glories of His kingdom upon the earth.

In the program of God periods of time

are allotted for the accomplishment of certain things, and at the end of those periods,
or ages, an invoice is taken of the spiritual
attainments and moral wealth of the race;
unjust stewards are called to an accounting,
and are punished, the good are promoted,
and a leaf is turned in the program of God,
a new and better age is inaugurated; it is a
harvest time when God gathers out the good
grain, subsoils the field of moral and spiritual endeavor, turns under the thorns and
briars and sows the good seed for larger and
better harvest. It would be interesting and
profitable if we could, with a good degree of
accuracy, locate ourselves in the movement
of God's times and know about where we
stand in the program of events, moving forward to the coming of His kingdom on
earth.

Let me illustrate: Suppose you are going to an entertainment; it is perhaps, the
close of the school year; it may be you are
deeply interested in what is to appear upon
the platform. You are detained by some accident; you arrive a half hour late at the
hall, or theater where the entertainment is
given; when you come in a printed program
is handed to you; you take your seat; the
actors are on the stage before you, but you
do not know what acts of the performance

have gone forward before your arrival, what part of the program is now being enacted, or who the performers are. You whisper to a friend near you for information; he points out to you the parts of the program that have been acted and what is now proceeding on the stage. This gives you an intelligent appreciation of the performance, and you know who is before you, and the part they are acting.

Would it not be a source of enjoyment, a genuine thrill for our intellectual and spiritual life, if God should so arrange the program of His plan of human redemption, and the bringing in of His kingdom, that we, searching the Scriptures, can definitely locate ourselves in the age in which we are living, and understand the performance now going on upon the stage of human history, and by God's good grace, perform our part, and with some degree of accuracy, know what is to follow. Pre-millennialists claim that all this is possible, that we are coming to a culmination of history, that we are approaching the end of an age, that to perform our proper part we must make haste to spread the gospel to all the world, that the great need of the times is not the erection of vast cathedrals, costing hundreds of thousands, and even millions of dollars, for the cultivation of denominational pride, but that by every possible means we should speed the spread of the gospel, that we should proclaim to all men that Jesus came once to redeem for Himself a bride, that that bride is made up of "whosoever will come," and that He will come again to gather that bride to Himself, His church, redeemed by His precious blood, ruled over in great glory, bringing all the kingdoms of the world beneath the sway of the scepter of His love.

I well remember when I was a small boy, during the progress of the Civil War in these United States, I took great interest in the marching of the armies which passed the home where I lived. In the armies of both the North and South there were certain celebrated regiments which had held in check the advancing foe against great odds until re-enforcements arrived. There were certain batteries that had protected a bridge, a hill-top against repeated charges of infantry; or there were squadrons of cavalry that had performed some daring and heroic deed. These regiments, batteries, and cavalrymen were the joy and pride of the army to which they belonged, and the cause they represented. I used to climb up on the yard fence, gaze upon the seared hosts, and ask with eagerness, "What regiment is this? Whose battery is that? To whose command does this cavalry belong?" On being informed, I felt a new and intelligent interest in the movement of the army. I knew something of the history and character of the men moving before me.

Pre-millennialists believe that God has a program; that it is set down in His word, that it is our privilege to study with care, and have some comprehension of the movement of events in the fulfillment of prophecy, that we may know, to some extent, what is passing before us, and this gives a splendid reality to things; it confirms our faith in the inspiration of the Scriptures; we feel that God has honored us, not only saving us from our sins through the merit of His Son, Jesus, but that He has taken us into His confidence, and that we may know something of where we are in the times which He has appointed.

Take, for example, the capture of Jerusalem by the British army in the World War, and the expulsion of the Turks, who have trampled Palestine under the feet of a barbarous despotism for centuries, the rapid return of the Jews, the improvements going forward in the ancient and sacred city of Jerusalem and throughout Palestine. To the Post-millennialist it has little or no significance. To the Pre-millennialist it is full of significance; it is the fulfillment of definite and repeated prophecies written in Old Testament history for thousands of years, and is a divine proof of the trust-worthiness of the Bible, and it is another event in the program of God that indicates to us that the coming of the Lord draweth nigh.

To the devout believer, who cherishes the "blessed hope" of the coming of our Lord, the prophecies and promises of His appearing in these times when skepticism is so widespread, so bold, and so defiantly ir-reverent, it is most comforting, and reas-sures the heart that God is faithful, that He will keep His promise, that Jesus Christ will appear in the clouds with His saints and the holy angels, that the dead in Christ will arise, that then the whole world, both saints and sinners, will be convinced that Jesus is the Christ, the only and all-suffic-ient Savior of men, and thus they are stimu-lated to obey that impressive exhortation of the Apostle Paul to his beloved Timothy, "That thou keep this commandment with-out spot, unrebukeable, until the appearing of our Lord Jesus Christ: which in his times he shall show, who is the blessed and only Potentate, the King of kings, and Lord of lords."

CHAPTER IV.

IS THE WORLD GROWING BETTER OR WORSE?

Is the world growing better, or is the world growing worse? is an old question and often asked. This is an interesting and serious question, and well deserves attention. It is reasonable and well, that now and then reading the Scriptures, studying human history, looking about us, and observing world conditions, that we ponder this question: Is the race making progress? Are we going forward or backward?

We have many answers to this question coming from various viewpoints; the opinions of the observer will have much to do with his conclusions. Much is embraced in a question covering so much history, and so large a space, that one should think long and soberly before coming to a positive conclusion, and undertaking a definite answer.

History reveals the fact that there come epochs when nations reach a climax of prosperity; the race goes forward in discovery, invention, and development to a certain point; then decay sets in; there is moral laxness, wealth accumulates, pride increases; there is luxury, idleness and wickedness. There is weakness of in-

tellectual and moral fiber. Women lose
their modesty and virtue; men become selfish and lustful; God is forgotten, His laws
are violated, His warnings are unheeded,
His mercies are rejected, and His judgments fall upon the people.

Sin brings its own penalty; it produces
decay; there is in it the nature of the can-
cer which eats away the life, the virus of a
subtle and certain destruction. The Babylonian empire was great. There were architects and artists; literature was developed,
a magnificent city was erected; into it
flowed the commerce of the pagan world,
but they reached the climax of wickedness
from which they fell headlong into destruction and total ruin.

Greece developed a magnificence unknown before, and scarcely surpassed in
history. She, too, became the master of the
world. Alexander, the young king, swept
all foes before him; the architecture and
art of Greece reached an acme of greatness,
but she, in her wickedness, following in the
footsteps of the nations preceding her, went
down in decay and ruin.

Rome became the mistress of the world;
founded upon her seven hills she seemed to
be unconquerable and impregnable. No
doubt, her architects, lawyers generals, art-

ists, and poets, believed that the world was growing better, and that they would abide and grow into higher heights of power and glory throughout the ages; but she reached the summit of her power, and fell into decay.

Thus it was with the Hebrew age. The calling of Abraham was full of promise; his family developed into a tribe, the tribe grew into a nation, the nation furnished the inspired men to write the Old Testament Scriptures. The Hebrew people rose to a power and eminence that attracted the attention of the nations of the earth. The climax was reached in the building of the temple in Jerusalem, and the glory of the reign of Solomon; then decay set in and was followed by stage after stage of retrogression until God's backslidden people built altars to idols; chastisements were sent upon them, the tide of spirituality ebbed and flowed until there came a fearful decadence which reached its climax in the rejection and crucifixion of the Lord Jesus, the destruction of Jerusalem, the captivity and scattering of the Hebrew people; and thus ended one of the great dispensations of time, which God had marked off in the history of the race.

The question arises, Will history repeat

itself? Modern civilization is perhaps no more secure than these ancient nations of whom we have spoken. Hasn't Spain long since reached the climax of her power and influence? Is it not quite improbable that she will ever even hope for the return of the glory of her empire? Germany had made most remarkable progress; she had reached a supremacy in practically all of the useful arts. Her commerce was making the most rapid progress. She was contributing largely, not only to the comforts of civilized people in her varied manufacturies, but was rendering splendid service along all lines of scientific discovery. But her great teachers attacked the inspiration of the Scriptures, questioned the Godhead of the Lord Jesus; her spiritual fires went out, her intellectual leaders forgot God, her scientific discoveries were devoted to the destruction of men and the baptism of Europe with an unprecedented scourge of fire and blood; and while she staggers beneath the financial burdens of an unheard-of war indemnity, her scientists are busy, as those of other nations, in seeking for implements for the more fearful destruction of human life, and devastation of civilization.

Many thoughtful people believe that Great Britain, as a nation, has reached and passed the climax of her power. She is no longer the center of the financial world; the spirit of agitation and rebellion is rife among the various peoples under the sway of her scepter. She has economic problems most difficult of solution; her wisest statesmen tremble with apprehension. None of them would undertake to forecast what the immediate future, in the way of radical changes, and the possible breaking up of the empire, contains for Great Britain.

And thus we might write of the nations of the earth; and it is not an idle question to ask, "If history will repeat itself?" If the nations of modern times will follow in the footsteps of those who have gone before us, and have gone down into decay and disappeared, leaving their magnificent ruins as tombstones over dead empires, and warnings to those who may come after, that God's mercy knows the appointed bounds, and turns to vengeance there.

Turning our thought to the great dispensations of grace, as we contemplate the question as to whether the world is growing better or growing worse? we find comfort in the fact that, while a dispensation, or an age, may grow and develop, making splendid progress until it reaches a climax of great prosperity, wealth and learning, and then decay sets in, and finally, the dispensation comes to disintegration and ruin, then God gathers out what saints He finds, destroys the sinners who will not repent and be saved; He always inaugurates a better dispensation. It is safe to say, that the Hebrew age was a vast improvement over the antediluvian age. Out of that age destroyed by the flood, God was able to bring only eight souls—eight grains of good seed corn with which to replant the human race. Divine light was greatly increased; the prophets came; Israel was brought into Canaan; they had with them the laws of Moses; Isaiah preached and promised a golden future. Ezekiel labored with faith and fervor, prophesied the scattering and restoration of Israel. David wrote the Psalms, Solomon the Proverbs. It was a great period in history. The spiritual comprehension of these ancient seers and kings, under the guidance of the Spirit of God, was most remarkable. There is no comparison between the antediluvian people and the Israelites, their enlightenment and progress along all lines of intellectual and spiritual development and achievement. In this particular, the world was growing better.

Repeating what we said before, decadence came; Israel backslid, true spirituality went out of the church; here and there was a faithful saint, but the chief men of Israel were blind leaders of the blind, and they fell together into the ditch of a fearful apostasy. But God was not to be defeated. Out of the wreck of Israel He gathered the material for the inauguration of a new dispensation; He kindled the fires of the gospel age. He organized and set up the New Testament Church, and sent forth His messengers to offer salvation by faith in a crucified and risen Lord, to lost men in all the world.

All thoughtful persons will admit that the gospel age is a vast improvement over the Hebrew age. The dispensation of salvation by faith in the Lord Jesus far surpasses the times of slaying bullocks and goats and lambs, and the tedious and burdensome religious ceremonies of the Hebrew age, all of which had their place and spiritual significance in the preparation for a larger revelation, and the better age of gospel grace and power. In this respect the world is growing better.

The inspired apostle has in mind the superiority of this age over the Hebrew age, when he says: "God, who at sundry times and in divers manners spake in time past unto the fathers by the prophets, hath in these last days spoken unto us by His Son, whom he hath appointed heir of all things, by whom also He made the world; who being the brightness of His glory, and the express image of His person, and upholding all things by the word of His power, when He had by Himself purged our sins, sat down on the right hand of the majesty on high." Heb. 1:1, 2, 3.

The coming of the Lord Jesus Christ was a climax of history; all of revelation, all of divine visitation, all of the teaching of prophets and priests, the building of altars, and the offering of sacrifices, had been pointing to the coming of the Lord and Saviour, His death to atone for the sins of the people, and His resurrection and intercession for the lost race, at the right hand of the Father. The Sun of righteousness has arisen in the gospel age, and with its brilliancy and glory throws into eclipse all that has gone before.

So we see that God is not fighting a losing battle; that out of seeming defeat He brings victory; and in this larger and better sense, His kingdom grows, and every succeeding dispensation is far superior to that which preceded it. Thus it has been, and will be. We are now living in the gospel age, a wondrous age of opportunity, gospel

grace and blessing; but we have been taught
to pray for the kingdom age: "Thy kingdom
come. Thy will be done in earth, as it is in
heaven." This prayer given to His Church
by our Lord, is full of prophecy and promise. We may be sure that the Lord Jesus is
not teaching us to pray for that which is
impossible, which cannot come to pass. This
answer was laid up in the storehouse of
heaven before Jesus taught His people to
offer the prayer. God's kingdom will come.
His will be done on earth; the kingdoms of
this world will become the kingdoms of our
Lord Jesus Christ.

Let us remember, and comfort our
hearts with the blessed optimism that our
Christ is winning, that He is ever moving
forward, that God cannot fail; that, although an age may become corrupt and, for
a time, there may be an ebb of moral forces,
and spiritual power, that when the climax
is reached God comes in, separates the good
from the bad. Sin brings its logical consequences; those who persist in wickedness
and refuse to repent, are punished, and the
saints of a decaying dispensation are
brought over and transplanted into a new
age which far surpasses anything in the
past. Satan is defeated and God goes forward with His loyal people from conquest

to victory. In this broad sense, the world
in its great aggregate, in its profound and
deepest significance, in its high and holiest
purpose, under the guidance of Almighty
God, goes from lower to higher level, from
worse to better conditions, from a decaying
age into a new age of greater light and ho-
lier living.

While we cannot insist, nor do we believe,
that our present age is improving in its
morals, or approximating in its spiritual
life anything like the possibilities under the
grace of the gospel and the guidance of the
Holy Ghost, and while we tremble for the
future, and are compelled to ask ourselves
what the outcome may be, as a result of the
skepticism, which is taught in the schools,
the unbelief which is preached in many pulpits, and the blasphemous infidelity scattered abroad by a godless press, the immodesty
of the times, the divorce, the breaking up of
families, the lawlessness, the desecration of
the Sabbath, and the high tide of sin about
us everywhere, yet we rejoice that we know
there is ahead of us a new and truly golden
age.   We know that our Lord will keep His
promise, that God has not forgotten the revelation He made to His prophets, that there
is coming a day of separation, of winnowing
the chaff from the wheat, of the appearing

of our blessed Lord and Master; and with joyful optimism we labor for the salvation of human souls, while we wait with glad expectation for the coming of our King, and the inauguration of an age that shall eclipse with its glory all ages that have passed; a consummation and gathering up into one age of all the good and holy men and women who have gone before, and have looked forward with hope and song to the glad and glorious period, when "the knowledge of the glory of the Lord shall cover the earth as the waters cover the sea."

An age may grow worse, but God keeps His promise. He sweeps away the accumulation of wickedness; He sends to the eternal prisonhouse those who will not be subject to His moral government; He brings over into a far better age those who have been faithful, and thus He ever goes forward with increasing power, an enlarged number of saints and followers, until His glorious plan is consummated, and His kingdom is set up upon earth.

With this broader view of the situation, taking in, not a section, but the entire world, not one period of history, but all history, not one age at its ebb tide of intellectual, moral and spiritual life, but all ages, with the accumulating good that God has brought out of them, there can be no reasonable question but that this Gospel Age is the best of all ages; in this larger and better sense the world,—by the use of the term world we simply mean the inhabitants of the earth— under the increasing light of God's love and grace has ever been growing better. Let the reader understand that, when an age becomes corrupt and apostate, God has a harvest time, destroys the evil and brings in a far better age, always looking forward to, and moving onward to "Thy Kingdom come; Thy will be done on earth as the angels do it in heaven," when Christ shall wield the scepter of love over all nations and tribes of all the earth, and a holy fraternity shall prevail among men, and they shall "learn war no more."

This writer believes we are now entering upon a period of materialism, love of wealth, pleasure seeking, unbelief, lawlessness, moral laxness, a spiritual decay, forgetfulness of God, love of self and sin, that will in all probability lead on into the apostasy of which the Apostle Paul speaks, which will evidently take place directly before the coming of our Lord. We believe the perilous times are coming upon us; of this we shall speak at length in another chapter. Let us watch and pray, and keep our lamps trimmed and burning.

CHAPTER V.

THE POWER OF THE GOSPEL.

There is a class of Post-millennialists who, in their arguments against, and ridicule of, the faith, longings and happy anticipations of Pre-millennialists, take pleasure in saying that those who rejoice in the hope of the soon coming of the Lord Jesus, believe that God having failed with the gospel to persuade men to repent and come under His divine government, must needs resort to force in order to set up His kingdom on earth.

Nothing could be farther from the facts in the case, than this accusation. Pre-millennialists have implicit faith in the power of the gospel to save those who believe in and accept its message of salvation; at the same time, they recognize the fact that there is no coercion in the gospel plan of human redemption. God does not use physical or any other force in order to compel men to be saved against their will. This is impossible; God uses persuasion, warning, entreaty; He reveals heaven and hell, holiness and sin, the final outcome of obedience to His commandments, of acceptance of salvation through faith in Christ, and of rebellion, wickedness, impenitence, and the rejection of all the means He has provided whereby men may be saved, and then He invites and urges men, in the light of all this revealed truth, to make their choice. This always has been, and always must be the divine method.

It is a fact that throughout the history of the Church a large percent of the people among the most highly civilized and best evangelized nations have always rejected the gospel. Let the reader select any city, town, or community, with which he or she is best acquainted, where the gospel has been preached from the earliest settlement of such population, where great revivals of religion have been held, where the people have had the largest and best opportunities of securing their souls' salvation, and it will be found that, notwithstanding all these means of grace, a very large percent of each succeeding generation has rejected the gospel and perished in their sins.

It is well understood that in all the teachings of Jesus and His apostles, and all true ministers of the gospel who follow after the example of the divine Master, and these first great preachers of the gospel, make the offer of salvation and urge men to make their choice. The salvation of the individual depends entirely on his own decision to repent and trust in Jesus for forgiveness, or to reject the offers of divine mercy, continue in his sins, and take the fearful consequences. Sad to say, the massses of humanity have, of their own free will, rejected the gospel and chosen sin and death.

It is very generally understood among intelligent, thoughtful Christians that judgments follow on the heels of mercy. God never resorts to force to make men good; that were impossible; but when men refuse to be good, and insist on trampling upon divine law, plunging deeper into rebellion and sin, and bringing disorder and confusion into God's moral world preventing the spread of the gospel and the salvation of their fellow beings ,then God may, and does, use force; those who will not accept mercy must suffer justice. This is the whole tenor of Bible teaching, and is in harmony with the fitness of things. God cannot forsake the order of His universe and turn His moral world over to a rebellious people, permitting them to bring on disorder and chaos which would wreck civilization and prevent the spread of the gospel and the offer of salvation to such as will accept mercy and be saved.

Those who believe the Scriptures are plainly taught, and must believe that there came a time in the history of the antediluvian world when the people, having rejected the last offer of mercy, were doomed to destruction. God could not force them into goodness, but He could force them off of the face of the earth. He could put an end to their rebellion which was only propagating a race to sink more deeply into sin and degradation, and bring on additional woe and ruin to humanity. The same is true of the conclusion of the Hebrew dispensation. The Hebrew people had persecuted and slain God's prophets; they had gone into idolatry; a fearful apostasy had fallen upon Israel, and the Church was utterly corrupt. Its leaders and highest officials were so dead and blind to all spiritual truth that they were quite ready to kindle the hatred, and urge on the mob which demanded and secured the crucifixion of the Lord Jesus. It was not pagan Romans who thirsted for the blood of the Christ; it was the leaders and officials of an apostate church; they had departed from God and His truth; they knew nor cared nothing of the divine program; they had selfish and ambitious programs of their own. In the rejection and crucifixion of Christ they reached the highest climax of wickedness; there was nothing left for them but God's judgments.

The judgments of God came upon the apostate Hebrew people swift and awful. Some of their ancient prophets had warned them of the coming of the Roman army in its merciless vengeance. The Lord Jesus when He stood weeping on the Mount of Olives, saw these messengers of God's indignation marching against Jerusalem, surrounding it with their impregnable cohorts, and bringing the most fearful destruction upon a people who absolutely refused to have mercy. Long ago, David had written into the hymns of Israel, "The Lord is merciful and gracious, slow to anger, and plenteous in mercy. He will not always chide: neither will He keep His anger forever."

God has created the universe; He has peopled this globe; He has revealed certain fundamental laws for its moral government; all of His commandments come out of His love. When He says, "Thou shalt not," He would prevent us from doing those things that bring to us hurt. When He says "Thou shalt", He directs us to those things that always bring to us blessing. He nowhere proposes to compel men to obey, but He fixes certain bounds over which they cannot pass. When they undertake to pass these bounds He issues warrants for their arrest and no one can escape the vigilant eye and strong hand of the high Sheriff of heaven who executes the command of Almighty God.

It is hardly to be supposed that the coming of Jesus will not bring calamity to those who have rejected all offers of mercy, and continue, by rebellion and wickedness, to heap up wrath against the day of wrath. His appearing would certainly be most embarrassing to those preachers and teachers who are denying His virgin birth, His Godhead, the miracles He wrought, the gospel He preached, and the blood atonement He made for the sins of the people. There is coming a time of confusion and disaster to an unbelieving, pleasure-loving, and godless multitude who trample with indifference upon the blood of the everlasting covenant, who not only refuse salvation through repentance and faith in Christ, but riot in their wickedness. When the Lord appears suddenly in His glory their rebellion will be stopped, their laughter and ridicule will turn to cries for rocks and mountains to fall upon them and hide them from the face of the Christ they have rejected, mocked and re-crucified. God's faithful children, who love and long for the appearing of their Redeemer and King, can easily afford to endure with patience the ridicule of the scoffers, and wait joyfully until our crucified and risen King shall appear in glory.

Our Lord Jesus nowhere in His teachings, nor the apostles nowhere in their writings, intimate that we shall ever reach a period during the gospel dispensation when all men will be brought into a state of obedience, but in every parable and saying of our Lord with reference to His second coming He points out the fact that there will be some virgins without oil in their lamps, some servants unprepared for the coming of their Master, some called to the Marriage Supper of the King's Son without the wedding garment. Our Lord says distinctly, "Many false prophets shall arise, and shall deceive many. And because iniquity shall abound, the love of many shall wax cold. But he that shall endure unto the end, the same shall be saved. And this gospel of the kingdom shall be preached in all the world for a witness unto all nations; and then shall the end come." Matt. 24:11, 12, 13, 14.

Mark you, the gospel is to be a witness, a witness to men of God's mercy, a witness in the defense of God against His accusers and enemies on the day of judgment; a witness to the fact that through the gospel God has offered the world salvation in Christ, and that those who are unsaved, who have heard the gospel, are without excuse. Jesus tells us that after this gospel has borne witness to all nations, the end shall come; not the end of the world, mark you, but the end of an age, the closing of a dispensation, the end of the tremendous influence, wreck and ruin wrought by the prince of the power of the air, the end of the rule of selfishness, ignorance and barbarism, the end of widespread, corrupt civil government; the end of greedy trusts, the vast aggregations of corrupt and useless wealth on the one hand, of wretchedness, poverty, and starvation on the other hand; the end of swaggering infidelity, blasphemous pride, shameless lust, lawlessness, indecency, and vice of every kind. The end of war, bloodshed, famine and pestilence, and the beginning of the reign of peace on earth, and good will among men.

CHAPTER VI.

THE FULFILLMENT OF PROPHECY.

The Bible carries within itself ample proof of its divine inspiration; this proof is not only shown in the superiority of its laws, its moral standards, its social adjustment, and deep spiritual teachings above all mere human literature, but its prophetic foresight and the remarkable accuracy with which the prophecies contained in the Scriptures have been fulfilled afford a positive and infallible proof that the Holy Scriptures were written by divinely-inspired men.

It was the purpose of God to give us a reasonable ground for our faith, a firm foundation upon which we could rest our beliefs and build our hopes of salvation, and a future state of blessedness. Infinite wisdom could not have divined a wiser plan than that revealed in prophecy and its fulfillment. It would have been impossible for the ancient prophets to have so accurately forecast the coming events of history without inspiration. They could not have so placed the cogs in the wheel of prophecy, that they would fit so perfectly into the cogs

57

of the wheel of history, if the Holy Spirit had not revealed to them the coming events of the future. The fulfillment of prophecy lifts the Bible entirely out of the realm of mere human guesswork or forgery, and places it upon a plain of divine inspiration entirely beyond the reach of successful contradiction.

This method of divine revelation makes it impossible for the Bible to grow old or obsolete. It is so written that it can never become merely a book of the past. Fulfilling prophecy, as the years go by, makes the Bible, not only a book of the past, but of today, and of tomorrow, and of all times, both past and future.

The devout student of the Holy Scriptures, standing on the mountain peaks of prophecy, and looking back along the highway of history, beholds with delight how accurately prophecy has been fulfilled, and through the prophetic telescope he examines world conditions, and looks forward to the march of events falling into harmony with what the seers of God saw and wrote down thousands of years ago. All of this gives him a foundation for his faith, which is unshaken and restful.

There is nothing more interesting in all literature, divine or human, than the prophecies in the Old Testament Scriptures concerning the dispersion of the Jews, and the accuracy with which those prophecies have been fulfilled. There is a story told of the old Emperor William, grandfather of the deposed Kaiser. It is said that during one of his campaigns, sitting by his camp fire at night, he said to his chaplain, "Chaplain, what is the best external proof of the inspiration of the Bible? Answer me in a word; not in an argument or discussion, but in a word." The story goes that the Chaplain saluted, and said, "Sire, the Jews!" "Ha!" said the Emperor, "That is splendid! you could not have given a better answer. The Jews, as we have them in the Bible, in prophecy, in history, and in the world today, are a powerful external evidence of the inspiration of the Holy Scriptures."

We do not know that this conversation took place. It is quite probable that it did; it certainly could have taken place, if so, the Chaplain gave an excellent answer, and the Emperor made a fine comment. God not only has a book called the Bible, but He has in the world a people called the Jews. The Bible, with its history of the past, its prophecies concerning the Jews, and the Jews as they exist scattered throughout the world today, with the marvelous, almost miraculous preservation of the purity of their blood, and the preservation of their identity is a powerful proof that they are indeed a peculiar people, that God has a definite purpose concerning them, and the remarkable movement toward their restoration to Palestine, at the present time, a fulfillment of prophecy before our eyes, ought to give pause to the destructive critic and great comfort and encouragement to the devout believer in the infallibility of the Word of God.

Could any one conceive of a better way, or any other method half so good to attract the attention and confirm the faith of intelligent, reasoning beings, than this prophetic method. This plan of God to inspire men to write certain predictions of future events in the general account of the conduct of nations, giving minute detail of transaction and incidents that were to occur hundreds and thousands of years after the predictions were written, and behold, we stand in the midst of time and find that these foretellings of the ancient Seers of God dovetail into the facts of history all about us; not only has this been true of the past years, but it is true of events which are coming to pass in the very times in which we are living. It seems to us that intelligent people could desire no better evidence, or have presented to them no stronger proof of the inspiration of the Word of God, than the remarkable fact that the prediction of the ancient prophets, who claimed to be inspired of God for the delivery of their message, have been fulfilled with remarkable accuracy, and are now being fulfilled before our very eyes.

It is well understood that the belief of devout Christians in the second coming of Christ is a subject, and always has been, for the profane ridicule of the blatant infidel. He neither believes in the first or second coming of Christ. It is generally understood that the modern liberalist of the destructive critic school does not believe in the glorious appearing and reign of our Lord Jesus. Such an appearing, in the nature of things, is entirely undesirable to him, and would doubtless, interfere seriously with his program. Modern liberalists are almost all, if not altogether, evolutionists, and they can get along very well with their theories of human origin, progress, history and destiny without any divine Christ, sacrificial suffering, first, or second coming of our Lord Jesus. His conceptions of Christ are very vague and out of harmony with the Scriptures. In this discussion, we have no argument or message for this type of person. They seem to have so little faith in the Scriptures, and to be so out of harmony with evangelical Christianity, as contained in Old Testament and New, that we can hardly conceive of a way of approach to them for the discussion of any vital subject of human salvation, and the ways of God with humanity, as revealed in the Bible.

It is perhaps, hardly fair to say that all modern liberalists are Post-millennialists. We are not able to locate them anywhere with accuracy; in fact, they have not located themselves, and a large percent of them are far more in sympathy, and in harmony with, the views of the outstanding infidels who have contributed most to the destruction of the Christian faith, the wreck and ruin of human souls, than they are in harmony with the views and spirit of the great and godly men who have contributed most largely to the spread of the gospel, and the evangelization of the world.

There are many devout Christians, persons to whom we give the right hand of Christian fellowship and brotherly love, without a moment's hesitation, who are Post-millennialists. They do not believe in the second coming of Christ before the final judgment to set up a kingdom of righteousness and peace in the world. No doubt, we can accuse them of being in bad company, for they are much more in harmony and fellowship in this particular, with the skeptical modernist, than they are with a large class of devout and zealous Christians who hold steadfastly to the inspiration of the Scriptures and look longingly and hopefully for the coming of the Lord.

We should not, perhaps, indulge ourselves in upbraiding the devout Post-millennialists because of their bad company, for we of the Pre-millennial faith certainly have a good deal of company who believe in the coming of the Lord and, at the same time, have extreme views, and preach doctrines that we regard as unscriptural and hurtful. We should like, however, to call the attention of our post-millennial friends to the fact that, the pre-millennial view makes our Lord Jesus wonderfully real. It it a stimulant to faith in these times when unbelief is so rampant and irreverent, and harmonizes with the teachings of our Lord, to watch and pray, and keep our lamps trimmed and burning that, when the Master comes, as He will come, suddenly, when the unbelieving world is neither prepared for, or expecting Him, we may meet Him with joy.

The student of prophecy must not overlook the fact that there are two groups of prophecy concerning the coming of our Lord Jesus into this world. One of these groups has to do with His first coming and suffering; the other group with His second coming, rulership and glory. In order to get an intelligent conception of the meaning of these prophecies they should be carefully divided and studied separately. Here is where the Jews, living in the days of our Lord upon earth, made their fatal mistake. They failed to "rightly divide the word of truth." They seemed to have overlooked the fact that there was one group of prophecies that told of the coming Messiah, His sufferings, crucifixion and death, and another group telling of His second coming and glorious reign. It will be remembered that, when Jesus walked with the two disciples on their sad journey to Emmaus, after they had told Him concerning Jesus of Nazareth, and His death, and the finding of the empty tomb by "certain women of our company," that Jesus spoke to them on this wise: "Then he said unto them, O fools, and slow of heart to believe all that the prophets have spoken: ought not Christ to have suffered these things, and to have entered into his glory? And beginning at Moses and the prophets, he expounded unto them in all the Scriptures the things concerning himself."

It seems that the Jews in the days of Christ on earth, even His disciples, had lost sight of these scriptures and, instead of looking for the Messiah who was to come, preach repentance, offer Himself as a sacrifice for sin, provide a gospel of redemption for the evangelization of the world, and the setting up of His kingdom of righteousness and peace and joy in the Holy Ghost in the heart of the individual, they were expecting a king to marshal his armies, break the Roman yoke from off their necks, overthrow their enemies, and establish a kingdom on earth that would surpass the power and glory of the reign of Solomon.

The Jews based this belief and hope on the prophecies concerning the coming and reign of Christ. They lost sight of the prophecies concerning the first coming of Jesus, His suffering and death, as completely as many Christians have lost sight of the prophecies of the second coming of Christ and His reign of peace and love. It was because of this fact that the Jews crucified Jesus, and it is because many Christians are concerning themselves with the prophecies of the first coming, and losing sight of the prophecies of the second coming, that they

ridicule and oppose the views and hopes of
their pre-millennial brethren; but far
worse, they get entirely out of harmony
with God's program as laid down in the
Holy Scriptures, and set up plans and programs out of harmony with God's great
plan. They go to building up antagonistic
ecclesiasticisms; they neglect the evangelization of the world, while they cultivate ecclesiastical pride; while millions of heathen
go without the gospel, they spend millions of
money building vast cathedrals and expen-
sive churches, creating offices, elevating
men into positions of control and dictation
in the church over their brethren, building
them palatial homes, and paying them im-
mense salaries, which not only has no warrant in the Word of God, but is contrary to
the whole spirit and teaching of Christ. If
God loved the world well enough to give His
Son to die for its redemption, no doubt, He
wants the lost world to know of His love,
and the redemption provided for it.

When the Lord Jesus laid down His evan-
gelistic program, He did not say, you shall
organize and build up vast ecclesiasticisms,
striving with each other for supremacy, seeing who can build the finest temples with the
tallest towers, but He urged His disciples to
go, to go at once, to go into all the world and

preach the gospel to every creature. The Christ of the New Testament is not pleased to have the cross, the emblem of His suffering and death, perched upon the tower of a church edifice costing half a million, or a million and a half of money, but He would have that cross carried by Spirit-filled, warm-hearted missionaries into heathen lands proclaiming the salvation He bought upon the cross for their sinful souls.

We do not believe that it would be cause for adverse criticism if we should call attention to a rather modern organization called the "Christian Alliance." It is made up of a devout people. It is not necessary that we fully endorse all their actions, or believe all the tenets of their creed, in order that we may admire their devotion and zealous missionary spirit. The Christian Alliance people are all very earnest Pre-millennialists. It is an interesting fact that they worship in cheap tabernacles, rented halls, and wooden sheds, but at the same time, contribute thousands of dollars for the spread of the gospel and send out scores and hundreds of missionaries to the ends of the earth, with no uncertain sound with reference to the inspiration of the Bible, and the blood atonement of Jesus, along with the glorious hope of His second coming to bring peace on earth and good will to men.

We think it is safe to say that if since the days of Martin Luther, Protestantism had have spent as little money in its home fields for architecture and large salaries for ecclesiastical officials, in proportion as these people of the Christian Alliance, and had at the same time, been as liberal and zealous for the spread of the gospel as they are, all heathen peoples, long ago, would have heard the good news that, "God so loved the world, that he gave his only begotten Son, that whosoever believeth in him, should not perish, but have everlasting life."

Pre-millennialists are sometimes, in a spirit of ridicule, called "star gazers", as if they spent their time in indifferent idleness with reference to world evangelization, gazing up into the heavens expecting to see the coming of Christ. Unfortunately, a few times in the history of the church, little groups of devout and misled people have set the time for the coming of the Lord and have gotten together waiting and looking upward for His coming to be disappointed, and to warn all others against a like mistake; even then, perhaps, they were better occupied, and more pleasing to the Christ, than multitudes of church members who scoff at the doctrine of His coming, and spend their time in dancing, gambling, wasting untold millions of the Lord's money upon their lusts and sinful pleasures.

There are multitudes of church members who are quite confident that their ancestors were apes, that much of the Bible is folklore, who are very liberal in their attitude toward the virgin birth, miracle power and blood atonement of Christ, who are boasting that they live in a "new age" of intellectual freedom, who might be benefited with a little upward looking and serious thinking on the subject of death, judgment day, and the future state. Nothing is farther from their thought or desire than that Christ should appear and call them to an accounting of their stewardship.

Dwight L. Moody, the world evangel, Hudson Taylor, who established the China Inland Mission, A. B. Simpson, who organized the Christian Missionary Alliance and girdled the globe with missionaries, Billy Sunday, who has preached to more people than any living man, and was one of the most powerful forces in closing the saloons of this nation, were not "star gazers"; the same may be said of at least two-thirds of the earnest evangelists who believe the Bible and exalt the Lord Jesus Christ as the only and all-sufficient Saviour, who are laboring day and night in this nation, and throughout the world, to win the lost to Christ, and whose hearts are warmed and thrilled with the blessed hope that the coming of our Lord draweth nigh.

These men, with a host of devout pastors, who are standing steadfastly against the tidal wave of modern liberal skepticism within the church, and untold thousands of consecrated lay people were, and are, students of the Scriptures; they believe the prophets were inspired of God, they rejoice to see the marvelous fulfillment of the predictions of these holy, inspired men all about them, and however dark the day, they are full of a holy optimism, believing that out of this darkening night of infidelity, false teaching, lawlessness, war, pestilence, and wickedness of every sort, there is soon coming the glorious dawn of the day and kingdom of our Lord and Saviour Jesus Christ.

CHAPTER VII.

PROPHECIES CONCERNING THE COMING OF CHRIST AND HIS KINGDOM ON EARTH.

All through the Old Testament Scriptures we find the promise that Jesus Christ should reign over Israel; that eventually He should occupy the throne of David. It will be remembered that when Jesus asked the Jews, "What think ye of Christ? Whose son is he? They said to him, The son of David." They gave this answer in the light of Old Testament prophecy that, God would raise up a Man of the seed of David to occupy his throne forever.

It was because of this common faith received from the prophets, that the disciples asked the Lord after His resurrection, "Lord, wilt thou at this time restore again the kingdom to Israel?" It was in fulfillment of prophecy that the people met Jesus as He approached Jerusalem, riding upon the ass's colt, with branches of palm trees, crying, "Hosannah: Blessed is the King of Israel that cometh in the name of the Lord." Jesus was, indeed, their unrecognized King. The superscription which Pilate wrote and put upon His cross was the truth: "This is the King of the Jews."

Jesus was their unrecognized King. According to prophecy, the time is coming when the Jews will fully recognize and acknowledge Him. The prophet Micah some seven hundred years before the shouts of the angelic choir startled the shepherds in their midnight watches over their flocks on the Judean hills, wrote, "But thou, Bethlehem Ephratah, though thou be little among the thousands of Judah, yet out of thee shall he come forth unto me that is to be ruler in Israel; whose goings forth have been from of old, from everlasting."

The first part of this prophecy has been fulfilled. Jesus has been born in Bethlehem; He has never yet been ruler in Israel. That part of the prophecy has yet to be fulfilled and will be, for God's word cannot fail. Isaiah, filled with the Holy Spirit, saw Christ and His coming kingdom, when he wrote, "For unto us a child is born, unto us a son is given: and the government shall be upon his shoulder; and his name shall be called Wonderful, Counsellor, the mighty God, the everlasting Father, the Prince of Peace. Of the increase of his government and peace there shall be no end, upon the throne of David, and upon his kingdom, to order it, and to establish with judgment and with justice from henceforth forever. The

zeal of the Lord of hosts will perform this."
Isa. 9:6, 7.

This is followed by another declaration
of the same character: "And it shall come to
pass in that day, that the Lord shall punish
the hosts of the high ones that are on high,
and the kings of the earth upon the earth.
And they shall be gathered together, as
prisoners are gathered in the pit, and shall
be shut up in the prison, and after many
days shall they be visited. Then the moon
shall be confounded, and the sun ashamed,
when the Lord of hosts shall reign in Mount
Zion, and in Jerusalem, and before his
saints gloriously." Isa. 24:22-23.

We cannot see how the prophet could use
plainer language foretelling the reign of of
our Lord Jesus in Jerusalem. Nothing of
this sort occurred at His first coming; it is
reserved for His second coming in glory and
power. It is useless to try to sweep this
prophecy away with some sort of a spiritual interpretation. No doubt, Isaiah saw,
by the inspiration of the Holy Ghost, exactly
what he wrote, and what we most steadfastly believe. This is what thrills us with a
holy optimism, and enables us to take up
with triumph another statement of Isaiah
as he looks with exultation to the coming
and reign of Christ. "He will swallow up

death in victory; and the Lord will wipe away tears from off all faces; and the rebuke of his people shall he take away from off all the earth: for the Lord hath spoken it. And it shall be said in that day, Lo, this is our God; we have waited for him, and he will save us: this is the Lord, we have waited for him, we will be glad and rejoice in his salvation." Isa. 25:8, 9.

Here the prophet is describing the blessedness that shall exist among men when Jesus shall overthrow all wicked and oppressive governments, and shall take charge of His world which He created, and "whose right it is to rule." He goes on further to describe this reign of peace and blessedness: "Behold, a king shall reign in righteousness, and princes shall rule in judgment. And a man shall be as an hiding place from the wind, and a covert from the tempest; as rivers of water in a dry place, as the shadow of a great rock in a weary land." Isa. 32:1, 2.

It would be difficult for the holy prophet to overdraw the picture. Only think how the return of our Lord would overthrow and destroy unbelief, curb wickedness of every kind, and bring peace and joy to the world. The resurrection of the Lord Jesus settles all doubt in the minds of His disciples, and all of His followers in all ages, with reference to His Godhead and power over sin and death and devils. His second coming in glory will conquer and compel His enemies to believe that the Jesus of Bethlehem and of Calvary arose from the dead, that He is the eternal Christ, the Son of God manifest in the flesh.

Isaiah catches a glimpse of the glory that shall exist in the world when he says: "And the ransomed of the Lord shall return, and come to Zion with songs and everlasting joy upon their heads: they shall obtain joy and gladness, and sorrow and sighing shall flee away." Isa. 35:10. The Lord Himself describing this wonderfnl state of blessedness,says: "For, behold, I create a new heaven and a new earth: and the former shall not be remembered, nor come into mind. But be ye glad and rejoice forever in that which I create: for, behold, I create Jerusalem a rejoicing, and her people a joy." Isa. 65:17, 18.

We might continue with quotations from Isaiah, Jeremiah, Ezekiel, and the minor prophets, but we would not weary our readers. Go read these prophets and notice how they triumph in the second coming and glorious reign of our Lord. Take, for instance, Micah, 4th chapter, 1st to 4th verses: "But in the last days it shall come to pass, that the mountain of the house of the Lord shall be established in the top of the mountains, and it shall be exalted above the hills; and the people shall flow unto it. And many nations shall come, and say, Come, and let us go up to the mountain of the Lord, and to the house of the God of Jacob; and he will teach us his ways, and we will walk in his paths: for the law shall go forth of Zion, and the word of the Lord from Jerusalem. And he shall judge among many people, and rebuke strong nations afar off; and they shall beat their swords into plowshares, and their spears into pruninghooks; nation shall not lift up a sword against nation, neither shall they learn war any more. But they shall sit every man under his vine and under his fig tree; and none shall make them afraid: for the mouth of the Lord of hosts hath spoken it."

Let those who are interested in Bible truth read the prophets and they will find that these wonderful predictions of the reign of Christ can no more be interpreted with some sort of a spiritual interpretation, leaving out the restoration of the Jews, the rebuilding of Jerusalem, and the glorious reign of Christ, than the prophecies concerning the scattering of the Jews into captivity, the destruction of Jerusalem, and the first coming and crucifixion of Christ can receive a spiritual interpretation. They were actual history; they have been fulfilled. The Jews were scattered abroad in the earth, Jerusalem was destroyed, Jesus did come and was crucified. These latter promises of His coming, the restoration of Jerusalem and the reign of our Lord, now in prophecy, will become history.

The prophecies of Zechariah are full of gracious promises of the restoration of Jerusalem and the reign of the Lord. Take the first chapter, 16 and 17 verses: "Therefore thus saith the Lord; I am returned to Jerusalem with mercies: my house shall be built in it, saith the Lord of hosts, and a line shall be stretched forth upon Jerusalem. Cry yet, saying, Thus saith the Lord of hosts; My cities through prosperity shall yet be spread abroad; and the Lord shall yet comfort Zion, and shall yet choose Jerusalem."

Follow this with the second chapter, fourth and fifth verses: "And said unto him, Run, speak to this young man, saying, Jerusalem shall be inhabited as towns without walls for the multitude of men and cattle therein: For I, saith the Lord, will be unto her a wall of fire round about, and will be the glory in the midst of her." Read with this the tenth, eleventh and twelfth verses: "Sing and rejoice, O daughter of Zion: for lo, I come and I will dwell in the midst of thee, saith the Lord. And many nations shall be joined to the Lord in that day, and shall be my people: and I will dwell in the midst of thee, and thou shalt know that the Lord of hosts hath sent me unto thee. And the Lord shall inherit Judah his portion in the holy land, and shall choose Jerusalem again."

It occurs to us that if these scriptures do not mean what they say, they should not be written here; but they do mean what they say. The inspired prophet is writing of what shall actually come to pass, and we of the pre-millennial faith are thrilled with holy optimism as we read these marvelous promises of what shall come to pass, we believe, in the not so distant future; but whether the years be few or many, we shall hold on to our faith, and rejoice in the fact that there is promised us a first and better resurrection, and whether we die soon or live long, we shall behold the King in His beauty, and Jerusalem, shall be the seat and center of His earthly government, the joy of the whole earth.

We do not wish to weary our readers

with quotations from the prophets, but many of them may be so occupied they will not have time to turn to the Bible, or some of our readers may be on the train, or otherwise engaged so they have no Bible convenient. For that reason, we shall continue to quote at some length, other prophecies in harmony with those already given, which establish and confirm our faith in the coming and reign of our Lord.

Please to read the following: "Thus saith the Lord; I am returned unto Zion, and will dwell in the midst of Jerusalem: and Jerusalem shall be called a city of truth; and the mountain of the Lord of hosts the holy mountain. Thus saith the Lord of hosts; there shall yet old men and old women dwell in the streets of Jerusalem, and every man with his staff in his hand for very age. And the streets of the city shall be full of boys and girls playing in the streets thereof. Thus saith the Lord of hosts; If it be marvelous in the eyes of the remnant of this people in these days, should it also be marvelous in mine eyes? saith the Lord of hosts. Thus saith the Lord of hosts; Behold, I will save my people from the east country, and from the west country; and I will bring them, and they shall dwell in the midst of Jerusalem: and they shall be my people, and I will be their God, in truth and in righteousness." Zech. 8:3-8.

The reader will please to note the statement contained in the third verse: "It is from the mouth of the Lord." The Lord Jesus Christ who once walked about Palestine preaching the gospel. "I am returned unto Zion, and will dwell in the midst of Jerusalem: and Jerusalem shall be called a city of truth; and the mountain of the Lord of hosts the holy mountain."

Of course, I understand perfectly well that our post-millennial friends will say that this does not mean that the Lord Jesus will actually and literally return to Jerusalem; but we question whether they have any scriptural authority for their statement. Why not? He did come to Jerusalem. He walked its streets, taught in its temple, and suffered crucifixion just outside its gates. He was then, just as He is today, the Son of God, co-eternal with the Father, the Creator of all things, absolutely perfect; absolute perfection cannot improve. Jesus is the "same yesterday, today and forever."

If He should come into Jerusalem upon an ass's colt to be reviled, thorn-crowned, spitted upon, and crucified, why should He not come again to Jerusalem on a cloud of glory to be received and adored by His redeemed people? He was the same Christ then that He is now. If He could condescend to such suffering to redeem the world, why should He not come back and manifest Himself for the rebuke of His enemies, the comfort of His people, and the setting up of His kingdom of righteousness and peace upon earth.

There is a wonderful promise and prophecy in the form of prayer He gave to His disciples: "Thy kingdom come; thy will be done on earth, as it is in heaven." When Jesus gave us that form of prayer to treasure in our hearts, to offer to the Father through the centuries, He had in His thought the fulfillment of the prophecies we have quoted in this chapter, and the setting up of His kingdom in the world. "And the Lord shall be king over all the earth: In that day shall there be one Lord, and His name one." Zech. 14:9.

Some of our post-millennial brethren have been wont to say that the doctrine of second coming and reign of Jesus rests upon one passage of scripture, and that that passage is found in the Book of Revelation; a book for which the modern liberalists have little, or no, respect, regardless of the fact that the beloved John opens up this book with this promise: "Blessed is he that readeth, and they that hear the words of this prophecy, and keep those things which are written therein: for the time is at hand." Rev. 1:3. He also closes this remarkable book with these words: "For I testify unto every man that heareth the words of the prophecy of this book, if any man shall add unto these sayings, God shall add unto him the plagues that are written in this book: And if any man shall take away from the words of the book of this prophecy, God shall take away his part out of the book of life, and out of the holy city, and from the sayings which are written in this book."

We are quite ready to admit that this Book of Revelation is filled with profound mystery, but we shudder at the thought of undertaking to ignore the blessing pronounced, and the warning given; we would forbear to undertake to explain away any of these things because they are deeper than our thinking, or higher than the reach of our understanding.

We call attention to the twentieth chapter of Revelation, and in order that the reader, who may not have a New Testament at hand, we quote at length: "And I saw an angel come down from heaven, having the key to the bottomless pit and a great chain in his hand. And he laid hold on the dragon, that old serpent, which is the Devil, and Satan, and bound him a thousand years, and cast him into the bottomless pit, and shut him up, and set a seal upon him, that he should deceive the nations no more, till the thousand years should be fulfilled: and after that he must be loosed a little season. And I saw thrones, and they sat upon them, and judgment was given unto them: and I saw the souls of them that were beheaded for the witness of Jesus, and for the word of God, and which had not worshipped the beast, neither his image, neither had received his mark upon their foreheads, or in their hands; and they lived and reigned with Christ a thousand years. But the rest of the dead lived not again until the thousand years were finished. This is the first resurrection. Blessed and holy is he that hath part in the first resurrection: on such the second death hath no power, but they shall be priests of God and of Christ, and shall reign with him a thousand years. And when the thousand years are expired, Satan shall be loosed out of his prison."

What shall we do with this plainly written word of God? It tells us that Satan shall be bound and cast into the bottomless pit for a thousand years. That is certainly good news. He has been making havoc in this world for many thousands of years; it would be a blessed thought and privilege to live in a world with Satan cast out of it. We are assured here that the righteous dead shall rise and reign with Christ a thousand years, in this first resurrection, in this reign of peace and glory, which the prophets have been foretelling.

No doubt, this is a troublesome revelation to our post-millennial friends, and is certainly of a character to lead the modern liberalist to insist on explaining it away altogether. There it stands, the word of God, the hope and joy of the Bride of Christ, through the centuries.

We have had the reign of Satan long enough. He has brought war, bloodshed, fire, destruction, pestilence and ruin among men. He cannot touch the eternal Father upon the throne of His universe, and he seeks to glut his hatred against Him in the destruction of the creatures He has created and loves; but the bounds are fixed, the time is appointed. As we approach the end of the age the Devil has "great wrath, because he knoweth that he hath but a short time." It seems that the devils who possessed unfortunate people in the days of Christ had some intelligence on this subject. In the record of the man possessed with devils dwelling in the tombs, as the Lord Jesus approached to deliver him, the devils cried out, "Saying, what have we to do with thee, Jesus, thou Son of God? Art thou come hither to torment us before the time?"

It seems that these devils who knew and recognized Jesus understood that the time for casting them out of the earth had not yet come. Jesus also recognized this fact, and instead of sending them into the bottomless pit, their final place of abode, permitted them to enter the herd of swine. It is a glorious thought that the time is coming when "that old serpent, called the Devil, and Satan, which deceiveth the whole world, shall be cast out of the earth," and deceive the nations no more.

This is the blessed hope of God's children, to whom the Bible is an inspired Book, who believe that the prophets spake under the guidance of the Holy Ghost, and rejoice in the fact that we are approaching a golden age in human history of which the poets have sung, for which statesmen have longed, upon which the inspired prophets fixed their enraptured vision, and for which the Bride of the Lord Jesus, His saved and sanctified church, has waited and prayed, and labored through the centuries. We can but join the beloved apostle in the conclusion of his inspired writing, and say, "Even so, come, Lord Jesus."

Reverting to this twentieth chapter of Revelation, from which we have quoted extensively, let it be remembered that this does not refer to the final judgment, but to the coming of Christ, and the inauguration of His Millennial Reign; after the thousand years are ended, Satan is to be loosed out of his prison and "shall go out to deceive the nations which are in the four quarters of the earth, Gog and Magog, to gather them together to battle: the number of whom is as the sand of the sea." After this battle the great white throne of the final judgment is set up, and all the multitudes of all human history are assembled at the great day of judgment.

It was the coming of Christ for the setting up of His kingdom, and this thousand years of His Glorious Reign, that Jeremiah saw and speaks of in the twenty-third chapter, fifth and sixth verses of his prophecy: "Behold, the day is come, saith the Lord, that I will raise unto David a righteous Branch, and a King shall reign and prosper, and shall execute judgment and justice in the earth. In his days Judah shall be saved, and Israel shall dwell safely; and this is his name whereby he shall be called, THE LORD OUR RIGHTEOUSNESS."

CHAPTER VIII.

THE SIGNS OF CHRIST'S COMING.

Our Lord Jesus in His teaching, constantly keeps before us the fact that no man knows, or can know, the day and hour of His coming. This was true of His first advent into the world; the Messiah was promised to the Hebrew Church, but the date of coming was never given; through the centuries the Hebrew people hoped, waited and longed for His appearing.

The faith they had, that He would come, was a powerful factor in binding them together, and keeping them a separate and distinct people. In their first dispersion and captivity they continued to turn their faces in their prayers toward Jerusalem, and no doubt, the burden of their prayers was the pleading of the promises of a coming Messiah. This hope inspired them through all the weary years of the captivity and suffering.

It is possible that, under their persecutions and severe punishment, "scattered and peeled," the Hebrew people might have given up their faith, mingled with other nations and lost their identity, but for this promise ringing a note of hope through all the prophecies of their inspired men that a Messiah should come. This promise and hope kept the fires of faith burning, held them together, and made them a peculiar and distinct people.

The same is true of the Christian Church; Jesus, her Lord and Saviour, before His departure, promised again and again, that He would return; He exhorted her to live in this "blessed hope," to keep her wedding garments ready, her lamps trimmed and burning. How natural that the betrothed bride should be busy preparing her wedding garment and with anxious joy looking forward to the coming of her Bridegroom. In the dark days of persecution, this blessed promise kept the fires of faith burning in the hearts of the persecuted and despised followers of the Lord Jesus, and today, amidst the skepticisms that have broken in upon the church, the floods of worldliness that are rampant in the sanctuaries of the Lord, the high tides of lawlessness and wickedness on every side, the true Bride of Christ comforts her heart that the coming of her Bridegroom draweth near. This undying belief nurtures her life, inspires her faith and courage for zealous service, while she waits for His glorious appearing.

While the date of the appearing of our Lord is kept secret, certain signs are given us to encourage our hearts, keep us hopeful and watchful, while we wait. Notice the words of the Master in Matthew 24:32, 33: "Now learn a parable of the fig tree; When his branch is yet tender, and putteth forth leaves, ye know that summer is nigh. So likewise ye, when ye shall see all these things, know that it is near, even at the doors."

We are taught here that certain things shall come to pass in the world, which are just as positive proof that the coming of the Lord is near, that it is "at the doors," as the buds on the fig tree indicate that summer is nigh. This teaching of our Lord certainly justifies a reverential study of the signs of the times; a devout inquiry into what has passed, what is passing, and what we may expect in the future, and thus, comfort our hearts with the hope that we are rapidly approaching the fulfillment of those prophecies which promise us a glorious period in human history when men shall beat their swords into plowshares, their spears into pruninghooks, shall learn war no more, and peace and happiness shall reign throughout the earth.

Devout men should not be accused of being pessimists because "seeing all these things" they are persuaded that from this time forward, events will move rapidly, prophecy will be fulfilled, Satan will be cast out, that deceiver of the nations, the fosterer of war, bloodshed, spread of disease and human woe, and Christ will return, and "the knowledge of the glory of the Lord will cover the earth as the waters cover the sea."

What are some of "these things" to which our Lord refers:

"Nation shall rise against nation, and kingdom against kingdom: and there shall be famines, and pestilences, and earthquakes, in divers places."

"Many false prophets shall arise, and deceive many. And because iniquity shall abound, the love of many shall wax cold."

"This gospel of the kingdom shall be preached in all the world for a witness unto all nations; and then the end shall come."

Jerusalem shall be destroyed, there shall be great suffering, Christ's disciples are to flee to the mountains for protection, "False Christs, and false prophets, shall show great signs and wonders; insomuch that, if it were possible, they shall deceive the very elect."

These are some of the things that were to take place prior to the coming of our

Lord; other things are spoken of by the prophets and apostles. The return of the Jews, at least in large numbers, to Palestine, and the great apostasy of which the apostle speaks, the running to and fro in the earth; and the increase of knowledge among men is spoken of by the prophet as taking place before the coming of the Lord.

"These things," which are to the times as the budding of the fig tree, have been fulfilled, or appear to us as being rapidly fulfilled. Jerusalem has been destroyed, the nations have fought and destroyed each other and are in preparation for yet greater conflict, false prophets fill the wide world with their teaching against the inspiration of the Bible, the virgin birth and deity of our Lord, offering all sorts of substitutes for regeneration and sanctifying grace for the individual, false Christs are offered to the people, and multitudes are wandering away after various men and women in absolute violation of the teachings of God's word, and fulfillment of what our Lord Christ teaches us would come to pass; the Jews are returning to Palestine, Jerusalem is being enlarged and rebuilt, and there is a widespread apostasy and departure from the Christian faith throughout the civilized world.

In Collier's National Weekly, Feb. 19,

1927, there appears a very interesting article written by a brilliant Japanese telling how he was converted to Christianity under the influence and ministry of Bishop Walter R. Lambuth, of the Methodist Episcopal Church, South. After concluding the excellent story of how he was brought to Christ, he makes this very interesting comment:

"And then I came to the United States. Here I have seen literally millions of Christians in perfectly good standing in the church take something of a pleasure in speaking unkindly of their richer neighbors. I have seen more millions of them entirely happy in revising the Sermon on the Mount to read, 'Lots of men can serve two masters. Ye can serve God and Mammon.' I have seen still more millions of equally excellent Christians take the name of God in vain— and in the jolliest manner imaginable.

"Here I have heard (although, of course, I don't believe a word of it) that the greatest city in this Christian America has smashed the world record for crime and that its expensively paved streets are buried under the broken fragments of the Ten Commandments.

"I have seen that old-fashioned thing— which we Japanese still think a good deal of—called parental control become a lost art among the Christian people in this country."

We shall not at this time comment directly upon these signs of the times, but turn our attention to a "sure word of prophecy; whereunto ye do well that ye take heed, as unto a light that shineth in a dark place, until the day dawn, and the day star arise in your hearts: knowing this first, that no prophecy of the scripture is of any private interpretation. For the prophecy came not in old time by the will of man: but holy men of God spake as they were moved by the Holy Ghost." 2 Peter 1:19, 20, 21.

We wish now to call attention to the prophet Daniel's interpretation of the great image which Nebuchadnezzar saw in his dream. It will be remembered that the head of this image "was of fine gold, his breast and his arms of silver, his belly and his thighs of brass, his legs of iron, and his feet part of iron and part of clay." The king in his dream saw "that a stone was cut out without hands, which smote this image upon his feet that were of iron and clay, and brake them to pieces. Then was the iron, the clay, the brass, the silver, and the gold, broken to pieces together, and became like the chaff of the summer threshing-floor; and the wind carried them away, that no place was found for them: and the stone that smote the image became a great mountain, and filled the whole earth." Dan. 2:32-35.

In the interpretation of this dream, Daniel tells King Nebuchadnezzar that he represents the golden head of this image, that there will arise after him another kingdom inferior, represented by the breast and arms of silver; a third kingdom represented by the belly and thighs of brass, and a fourth kingdom represented by the legs of iron. Then the kingdom shall be divided into various kingdoms, represented by the feet of the image, which are part of iron, and part of clay, representing a number of nations ruled over by different kings. Then the stone cut without hands appears, breaks up the image into fragments, and becomes a great mountain filling the whole earth.

It is at this time of the breaking up of feet, in fact, the entire image, that Daniel says: "And in the days of these kings shall the God of heaven set up a kingdom, which shall never be destroyed: and the kingdom shall not be left to other people, but it shall break in pieces and consume all these kingdoms, and it shall stand forever.

"Forasmuch as thou sawest that the stone was cut out of the mountain without hands, and that it brake in pieces the iron, the brass, the clay, the silver, and the gold; the great God hath made known to the king what shall come to pass hereafter: and the dream is certain, and the interpretation thereof sure." Dan. 2:44, 45.

We should like to ask the reader if he can discover any harmony between this prophecy of Daniel and that contained in Isaiah 9:6 and 7? "For unto us a child is born, unto us a son is given: and the government shall be upon his shoulder: and his name shall be called Wonderful, Counsellor, The Mighty God, The Everlasting Father, The Prince of Peace.

"Of the increase of his government and peace there shall be no end, upon the throne of David, and upon his kingdom, to order it, and to establish it with judgment and with justice from henceforth even for ever. The zeal of the Lord of hosts will perform this."

We must beg the reader's patience while we follow the above with a quotation from Jeremiah 23:5 and 6: "Behold, the days come, saith the Lord, that I will raise unto David a righteous Branch, and a King shall reign and prosper, and shall execute judgment and justice in the earth. In his days Judah shall be saved, and Israel shall dwell safely: and this is his name whereby

he shall be called, THE LORD OUR RIGHTEOUS-
NESS.

We are aware that these scriptures appear elsewhere in this volume, but we like
to associate them closely together. There
is one more that we must add to them: "And
I saw thrones, and they sat upon them, and
judgment was given unto them: and I saw
the souls of them that were beheaded for the
witness of Jesus, and for the word of God,
and which had not worshipped the beast,
neither his image, neither had received the
mark upon their foreheads, or in their
hands; and they lived and reigned with
Christ a thousand years." Rev. 20:4.

In the light of these quotations from the
prophets, it is perfectly safe to say that,
whatever the modern liberalist may believe,
or the conservative Post-millennialist may
teach, the inspired prophets of the Old Testament Scriptures believed that God would
set up a kingdom, especially his own, on the
earth, and that the Christ of Bethlehem,
Gethsemane, and Calvary would be the
reigning King upon the throne of this kingdom.

But what about Nebuchadnezzar's dream
and Daniel's interpretation of it? Have his
prophecies been fulfilled? There is nothing
more plainly written in history than that

the head of the image, the Babylonian Empire, has been destroyed. This was followed by the Medo-Persian Empire, represented by the silver breast. This, too, was overthrown by Alexander the Great and followed by the Grecian Empire represented by the loins of brass. This was destroyed, and succeeded by the Roman Empire represented by the legs of iron which, in perfect harmony with the prophecy of Daniel, was broken up into a number of kingdoms, mixed with strength and weakness, represented by the feet of the image made of mixed iron and clay. These prophecies have been so remarkably fulfilled that we feel fully justified in believing that the prophecy of the "little stone" which represents the Kingdom of Christ, the breaking up of worldly kingdoms, and the setting up of the universal kingdom of God, will be fulfilled.

It is the accuracy with which the prophecy of Daniel is corroborated by history, that makes him the special object of assault by the destructive critics. To admit that Daniel lived and wrote his prophecies at the time claimed for him by orthodox Christians, is to admit that the Bible is inspired, and that your destructive critic cannot, and will not, consent to do. We, of the

pre-millennial faith do not hesitate to believe that Daniel was inspired, that God
enabled him to look with marvelous accuracy into the future and to write down
the things which were to come to pass, and
that up to the feet of the image his prophecies have been fulfilled with absolute cer-
tainty.

Where are we now in the image? In its
feet, to be sure. What are the conditions of
the feet? Are there not very strong and
serious indications of the breaking up of
kingdoms? Is there not at the present time,
a very strong prejudice against crowned
heads? A number of thrones have been
overthrown; the strong trend in the realm
of the old Roman Empire is toward social-
ism, worse still, toward communism. Kings
are becoming mere puppets; their premiers
are wielding the scepter of power. Kingly
authority is passing away from the earth;
governments are breaking down; the spirit
of rebellion, revolt and anarchy is in the
world. Nations are being crushed beneath
an almost unbearable taxation for the paying of war debts and the supporting of vast
armies; "Men's hearts failing them for
fear, and for looking after those things
which are coming on the earth."

There is a widespread feeling among

thoughtful statesmen and reflective people, everywhere, that we are rapidly approaching a crisis in human history. The problems of civilization embracing Oriental questions, questions of the Near East, labor and capital, social questions, marriage and divorce, are of such character that men can but wonder if there is any power to place a brake upon the downward trend toward a fearful catastrophe of civilization.

The students of history who believe the Bible, and watch prayerfully the rapid fulfillment of prophecy, are derisively called "Pessimists" because they can but see that we are approaching the darkening night of human disaster, which has always come at the close of an apostate and wicked age, before the morning break of a new and better age. These distressing conditions are but the onrush of human folly and wickedness that must come, according to the teachings of the infallible Word of God, immediately before the glorious appearing of Jesus, our Saviour, King of kings, and Lord of lords.

CHAPTER IX.

THE FALLING AWAY.

In the chapter preceding this, we find that we are now living in that period of history represented by the feet of Nebuchadnezzar's image, and that it was at this period the division of the empire into kingdoms should occur, and be followed by the breaking up of these kingdoms, that the God of heaven would set up a kingdom in the world, and that it should be permanent and abiding; according to John in Revelation, it shall last a thousand years, a Millennium, the period of Christ's reign on earth, toward which Pre-millennialists with a joyful optimism, look forward while they labor to bring the gospel to all the world.

The Apostle Paul was a prophet, a foreteller as well as a forth-teller. He has much to say of the coming of the Lord Jesus in his two epistles to the Thessalonians. The chapters of this first epistles so divided that the closing verses of each chapter contain most hopeful and gracious exhortations with regard to the coming of our Lord and Saviour.

In his second epistle to the Thessalonians he encourages the hearts of the believers with the assurance that "God will recompense tribulation upon them that trouble you; and to you who are troubled rest with us, when the Lord Jesus shall be revealed from heaven with his mighty angels, in flaming fire taking vengeance on them that know not God, and that obey not the gospel of our Lord Jesus Christ. Who shall be punished with everlasting destruction from the presence of the Lord, and from the glory of his power; when he shall come to be glorified in his saints, and to be admired in all them that believe." 2 Thess. 1:6-10.

It is because Pre-millennialists believe these plain writings of the apostle, and that the coming of the Lord will be a time of confusion to those who have rejected Him, and a punishment and overthrow to those who have denied His Deity, His blood atonement, and have arrayed themselves against the word of God, and the Son of God, that they are called pessimists, and have been accused of having a gloomy and pessimistic outlook with regard to the future. The same accusation may be made against the Apostle Paul; we simply believe his statements. It will be remembered that when our Lord Jesus stood before the high priest with His accusers on the day of His mock trial, and the high priest said to Him, "I adjure thee by the living God, that thou tell us whether thou be the Christ, the Son of God, Jesus saith unto him, thou hast said: nevertheless I say unto you, Hereafter shall ye see the Son of man sitting on the right hand of power, and coming in the clouds of heaven." Matt. 26:63, 64.

It was then that the high priest rent his clothes, and declared that Jesus had spoken blasphemy, and that no farther witness was needed. It was then that the gathering of the enemies of Christ declared "He is guilty of death." It was this good confession that He was the Son of God, and that He would appear in the clouds of glory, that sent Jesus to the cross. No doubt, the high priest and his associates regarded this statement of Christ as most pessimistic, indeed, a gloomy outlook, so far as they were concerned.

Our post-millennial friends have undertaken to make much of the statement of the Apostle Paul in which they claim he tried to check any influence that former writings of his had had on the subject of the second coming, and it is quite probable that the Apostle did see that some of the Christians were expecting Jesus too early, before certain programs of the Lord could be carried out; the gospel preached to all the world, and many prophecies fulfilled; but Paul, by no means, retracts any of his teachings with reference to the second coming; he simply gives them a word of caution. Here are his exact words: "Let no man deceive you by any means: for that day shall not come, except there come a falling away first, and that man of sin be revealed, the son of perdition; who opposeth and exalteth himself above all that is called God, or that is worshipped; so that he as God sitteth in the temple of God, showing himself that he is God." 2 Thess. 2:3, 4.

The Apostle here is not retracting any former statement; he is not surrendering the doctrine of the coming of our Lord, but he is giving words of caution and assuring the Christian that certain things shall occur before the appearing of the Lord. It is in this chapter that Paul gives his prophecy with reference to the coming of that person who is generally called the "Man of sin." "And then shall that Wicked be revealed, whom the Lord shall consume with the spirit of his mouth, and shall destroy with the brightness of his coming: Even him, whose coming is after the working of Satan with all power and signs and lying wonders, and with all deceivableness of unrighteousness in them that perish; because they received not the love of the truth, that they might be saved, and for this cause God shall send them strong delusions, that they should believe a lie: that they all might be damned who believe not the truth, but had pleasure in unrighteousness." 2 Thess. 8:9-12.

We wish to suggest that the Apostle Paul is not for one moment indicating that the first coming of our Lord, the atonement He made upon the cross, and the sending forth of His gospel, was to be a failure; by no means so. But he is pointing out a great apostasy, and the fearful consequences that will come to those "because they receive not the love of the truth, that they might be saved." Let it ever be kept in mind that God nowhere proposes to destroy a man's will power and force him into salvation. He offers forgiveness, He provides salvation, He urges men to repent; He issues the great call of "whosoever will", and He promises by the lips of His own Son that, "Whosoever cometh unto me, I will in no wise cast out." But the Scriptures teach that those who refuse His mercy, trample upon His laws, and oppose themselves to all His offers of grace, will be given over "to believe a lie." It is a dangerous thing, according to the Apostle Paul, to refuse to love the truth, and to have pleasure in unrighteousness.

We have many strange and "strong delusions" in the world today. Take Christian Science, with its denial that there is any such thing as sin, sickness, or death; that there is a devil, or that there is a hell or place of future torment. Can one conceive of greater contradiction of plain gospel teaching? They take bold and positive issue with the plain words of our Lord Jesus, and a large percent no doubt, a large majority, of the members of this peculiar cult, were once members of orthodox Christian churches, but they have fallen under the "strong delusion" of a widespread apostasy from the true faith of a vital gospel, and a gracious Christian experience. The same may be said of the followers of Russell. While these unfortunate people have much to say with reference to the coming of the Lord, they associate this doctrine with so much that is grotesque, unreasonable and unscriptural, that they bring reproach upon whatever truth they may have mingled with their error.

Is it not quite probable that the whole doctrine of evolution is a "strong delusion?" There is one thing certain: the great scientists who have been advocates of the theory of evolution, have been dangerous skeptics; their teaching and influence have wrought fearful havoc against evangelical saving faith, and perhaps, every brand of evolution has a strange mixture of skepticism with their adulterated Christian teaching. One thing is absolutely certain: evolution, as it is being taught today in the high schools, and most all of the colleges and universities in these United States, is producing a state of mind strongly antagonistic to evangelical faith, and is bringing up a generation of people almost impossible to evangelize, to bring to true broken-hearted repentance for their sins, and a faith in Christ which brings regeneration and consciousness of salvation.

It would be impossible for us to enumerate the false teaching spreading everywhere antagonistic to the gospel, the biblical plan of human redemption; and it has come to pass that revivals of religion, as they were known in the evangelical churches a half century ago, are almost unknown today. There are many revival meetings, great union gatherings, and drives for church members, but repentance, the forsaking of sin, the seeking of Christ, regenerating power, and sanctifying grace, as once known and experienced among the people, is largely disappearing.

The teachings of the destructive critics

have not only had a fearful effect in their opposition to the simple evangelical faith in Germany, England, and other countries of Europe largely dominated by Roman Catholicism, paralyzing to a sad extent, any sort of Protestant movement in those countries for real evangelism, but they have spread as a great religious plague throughout this nation. The seed was being sown with a degree of caution before the World War broke out but the enemy has become bold and defiant since that tremendous tragedy, and to be popular today, the minister of the gospel in all of our Protestant churches must, at least be "tolerant" toward a teaching that robs the Bible of its authority, Jesus Christ of His virgin birth and deity. There is sad lament everywhere over the lack of the positive note in present day preaching. Undoubtedly, there are many ministers who, like certain priests in the days of our Lord on earth, loved the praises of men rather than the approval of God, and they are not preaching that gospel which has power to kill and make alive for fear they will not be regarded as scholarly, and abreast with the progressive men of the times.

There is much bold, open, false teaching against the inspiration of the Scriptures,

the virgin birth, and the deity and blood
atonement of Christ. This departure from
the truth is remarkable in England, among
some of the bishops of the Episcopal
Church; and in this country men of promi-
nence do not hesitate from the pulpit to as-
sail the vital doctrines of redemption, as set
forth in the Scriptures. As one looks upon
this apostasy he is reminded of St. Paul's
First Letter to Timothy: "Now the Spirit
speaketh expressly, that in the latter times
some shall depart from the faith, giving
heed to seducing spirits, and doctrines of
devils; speaking lies in hypocrisy; and having their conscience seared with a hot iron."

The boldness and defiance with which
many ministers in our most evangelical
churches are speaking and writing against
the plainly written word of God, and the
very general reception and approval with
which their teachings are received, is positive proof that we are in a fearful state of
apostasy. A prominent evangelist said to
me not long since, that it seemed that the
average congregation is quite willing that
the destructive critics should preach most
dangerous heresies in their pulpits, but are
not willing that these false teachers should
be answered by those who hold steadfastly
to the word of God. We find ourselves in

this peculiar and embarrassing situation. The church has certain programs that call for the collection of large sums of money, and those who would cry out against these false teachings, and insist on the proclamation of the word of the Lord, are warned that their ministry has a tendency to alarm the people and prevent making contributions to the church, forgetting that these contributions will assist to carry forward programs which have in them a propaganda of false teaching that paralyzes spiritual life and destroys saving faith in church schools and mission fields. In other words, we must not speak a word against false teaching or we shall hinder the plans and programs of men who are more anxious to get the people's money for their church enterprises than they are to save the people's souls, and protect the fold of Christ against the ravages of wolves in sheep's clothing.

Your destructive critic comes along posing as a great scholar, boasting of his scientific knowledge, and preaching the very same infidelity that has damned countless millions of souls through the centuries, and we are cautioned to let him and his teachings alone, that he is in a realm that belongs exclusively to the scientific scholar; and prominent officials in the church seek to in-

timidate the faithful men of God, vociferat-
ing that, "this is no time for theological discussion"; that we must not stop to defend
the truth against these false teachers, but
we must keep busy making and giving our
money to send forth this same brand of
teachers to the mission fields, to despoil
evangelical, saving faith in our institutions
of learning.

The standing of the preacher in the average church does not depend upon his faithfulness to the word of God, his insistence for
regeneration, a pure heart and a holy life,
but upon the number of people he can bring
into the church, and the amount of money he
can raise, regardless of the fact that these
persons are brought in without any indica-
tion of true repentance and saving faith in
Christ, and, sad to say, the money that may
be raised by all sorts of questionable meth-
ods, instead of coming by the tithe and free-
will offerings.

It is high time that men in the pulpit
should give careful heed to Paul's exhortation in his Second Epistle to Timothy: "I
charge thee before God, and the Lord Jesus
Christ, who shall judge the quick and the
dead at his appearing and his kingdom:
preach the word; be instant in season, out of
season; reprove, rebuke, exhort with all

longsuffering and doctrine. For the time will come when they will not endure sound doctrine; but after their own lusts shall they heap to themselves teachers, having itching ears; and they shall turn away their ears from the truth, and shall be turned unto fables. But watch thou in all things, endure affliction, do the work of an evangelist, make full proof of thy ministry." 2 Tim. 4:1-5.

How applicable are these words of the Apostle to the times in which we are living. It is the great city churches with their supposed learned preachers that type the church life, set up the spiritual standards and direct the efforts and energies of the various denominations. We are thankful to God that among these churches there are numbers of pastors, faithful and true, who are standing valiantly for the word of God and the deity of Christ against the onslaughts of false teaching and worldliness, but we have large numbers of great churches with false prophets in their pulpits, who are pleasing the "itching ears" of an unregenerated or backslidden church membership, with all sorts of false doctrines. I think it will be generally admitted that there is a strange and sad timidity in the ranks of the ministry. Men are inclined to boast that they are not dogmatic in their preaching, which means that they are not positive, that they do not speak with authority, that they are hesitant and not quite sure of themselves and their message.

What is the effect of the teachings of the destructive critics who have clouded evangelical faith throughout Christendom? What is the effect of the teaching of evolution in the colleges and universities in all lands, and especially, in the public schools of these United States? What is the effect of the uncertain sound in the pulpit with reference to the inspiration of the Scriptures, the deity and saving power of our Lord Jesus? We ask these three questions because there is the closest kinship existing between this trinity of propaganda so widespread; it is destructive of evangelical saving faith; it all has a tendency to put God far away; it minifies Jesus as a person, as God manifest in the flesh, as the one, and only one, who is able to save sinners; it magnifies the conceit and pride of men, and produces everywhere a fearful spiritual dearth, breaks down the barriers of reverential fear of God, and spreads abroad worldliness in the church, and lawlessness in the world.

We must turn again to the Apostle Paul for a description of conditions brought about by the false teachers, and the fearful apostasy that, like a creeping paralysis, is coming upon us. "This know also that in the last days perilous times shall come. For men shall be lovers of their own selves, covetous, boasters, proud, blasphemers, disobedient to parents, unthankful, unholy, without natural affection, trucebreakers, false accusers, incontinent, fierce, despisers of those that are good, traitors, heady, high-minded, lovers of pleasures more than lovers of God; having a form of godliness, but denying the power thereof: from such turn away." 2 Tim. 3:15.

What a graphic picture the inspired apostle draws before us of existing conditions all about us. One might fill a volume in the discussion of these few verses of the old Apostle to his son Timothy. We can notice them but briefly. Let us bear in mind that in the Epistle to the Thessalonians and to Timothy the Apostle has in mind the coming of the Lord, the appearing of the Antichrist, and the apostasy which will fall upon the church as we approach the end of the age. We can but believe that in the expression "the last days," the Apostle has in his thought the closing period of the Gospel Age, the approach to the end of the time just prior to the coming of our Lord to set up His kingdom among men. He tells us that men shall become "lovers of their own selves, covetous, boasters, proud, blasphemers."

Is this not startlingly true of the times in which we are living? The covetous spirit is prominent everywhere. Take, for instance, the great trusts, the greed that is manifested. Groups of millionaires are organized throughout the world to control the necessaries of life. Take the coal barons; they have bought up, and control those parts of the earth that produce fuel; they fix the prices of labor and the sale of the products of labor, and are masters of the situation. They live in palaces, they revel in luxury, while those who risk their lives underground to produce their wealth, live in miserable huts, in many instances, with poor sanitary conditions, and their labor is so manipulated that a large percent of their time they cannot work at all. In order to keep up the price of coal, the mines are shut down, the laborers and their families are in dire want and become objects of charity, while the owners squander their millions in marriages, divorces, sailing the seas in palaces, and building magnificent homes in different countries, with many of those homes a large part of the year shut up and kept only by servants, while they luxuriate about the world. And thus, we might go forward with comment on present day covetousness.

One great trust controls the oil, another the lumber, another cement, another dressed stone, another the meat products, another the grain, another the cured fruit, another the fresh fruit, another the wool, another the cotton, and so we might go on indefinitely. The spirit of covetous greed is manifested everywhere, the rich growing richer, more insolent and proud, the poor growing poorer, more discontented, threatening and lawless. Perilous times have come.

Follow the Apostle farther; he tells us that children shall become "disobedient to parents, unthankful, unholy." The disobedience of children is one of the most notable and startling facts of modern times. It is so patent that we need not stop to argue here. It is seen and known on every hand. We hear much of "The revolt of youth", and it is understood that this is a revolt against parental government, and school discipline, and indeed, against civil government; we might go farther and say, a revolt against decency, modest dress, and virtue. Only think of the millions of young men in this nation found unfit for service in the World War because of disease brought on by immoral conduct. Undoubtedly we are living in times when a large percent of our young people are not only disobedient to their parents, but they are in rebellion against God; they have been taught in their schools, and many of them in Sunday school classes and from pulpits, that they may have very loose opinions with reference to the inspiration and divine authority of the Scriptures, and loose ideas about the virgin birth and deity of our Lord. One can but ask, what about the second crop of these young people who are disobedient to parents, careless of their marriage vows, who are fond of believing that their ancestors were apes, what sort of children will they produce? What kind of homes will they build up? What are we to expect of the children whose parents were disobedient children?

We are startled that in Russia the law should forbid any sort of religious teaching until the children are eighteen years of age. They are not allowed to attend church, and there must be no religious instruction in their school or homes, meanwhile, they are growing up in a high tide of skeptical teaching and immorality all about them. In a few years this unchurched, untaught, generation of young people will be the men and women of Russia. If the present Russia is seeking to break down civil government throughout the world and embroil the world in strife and war, what will the Russia of the immediate future be, and what may we expect of them as being in any way a contributor to world peace, and the progress and uplift of humanity.

We hold up our hands in horror at conditions in Russia, but what about our own land, with our teaching of a skeptical evolution, with the taint of a dangerous unbelief in our text-books, and almost all universities dominated by a spirit of antagonism toward evangelical Chrisianity. The apostle tells us that this disobedient, unthankful people will be "unholy." What about the present attitude toward holiness, the holiness that is secured through the cleansing blood of Christ? There is no holiness apart from the holiness that is provided in the atonement of Jesus, that is inwrought by the power of the Spirit through the cleansing of the blood of Christ. To thus preach holiness is to raise an outcry of objection, and to bring a spirit of ostracism and persecution, not only in the world at large, but in the church itself. One would think that the plain declaration in the word of God that, "Without holiness no man shall see the Lord," and "The blood of Jesus Christ his

Son cleanseth us from all sin," and that those who "hunger and thirst after righteousness shall be filled," would settle all debate on this all-important question. Nay, verily. Let any man preach to the average great city church, or village church, for that matter, that God requires holiness, that Christ in His death and resurrection, provides for holiness, that before men can enter into heaven, they must be cleansed from all sin through faith in Jesus Christ, and he will meet with a storm of protest, not from the outside world, but it will be raised within the church; high officials will be notified, pressure will be put on, and the preacher of holiness of heart, through the cleansing blood of Christ, will be quieted, or humiliated and persecuted.

Notice the apostle in his description of the people during these perilous times; he says they are "without natural affection, trucebreakers, false accusers, incontinent, fierce, despisers of those that are good." Will not this description, "without natural affection," apply to the breaking up of homes by divorce, the general disregard of marriage vows, and the widespread refusal of those who are married to bear and care for children? Is not the love of dogs, monkeys, and various animals, instead of babies, a manifestation of unnatural affection; and is not the tirade of brilliant literary men, who turn themselves into hyenas, opening the graves of the honored dead, and dragging forth their supposed sins and exhibiting them to the public, a manifestation of the same spirit that would dethrone God, rob Christ of His deity, and men of their saintliness, and all nobility of character, an outbreaking of hatred against the good, a disposition to pull down all men and standards to a low level of immorality and wickedness.

Note the apostle's comment: "Lovers of pleasures more than lovers of God." How applicable this to our times. The spirit of pleasure-loving is not content to remain in the world with its indecent and lustful dances, embraces, and vulgar enjoyments, but it breaks into the very church; the church building becomes an amusement hall, a restaurant for feasts, frolics of worldliness, and dancing. Perhaps there has never been a higher tide nor a more reckless revelry of love of pleasure and daring adventure into unholy realms of lust than at the present time in these United States, and in fact, throughout the civilized world. Startling to contemplate. The apostle tells us that these pleasure-lovers have a "form of godliness, but deny the power thereof." You may be sure that the multitudes who are brought into the church without repentance, without regeneration, and are being taught that they must not expect to be saved from sin, that no one can be really pure in heart and holy in conduct in this life, have no knowledge of the power of godliness. Not only so, but they deny that there is any such power. They know nothing of the preciousness of the pardoning mercy, or the cleansing blood, of the baptism, witness and abiding of the Holy Ghost. They excuse their sins and, having no comfort or joy in salvation, they continue to seek the pleasures and amusements of the world, which are utterly antagonistic to the spirit of denial of self, the taking up of the cross, and following after Christ.

No doubt, some one will say that this is a pessimistic view of the situation. It is a correct view. These facts stand out before us in bold relief, everywhere. The wicked admit that these conditions exist, and they glory in their existence. The righteous look upon them with grief and are vexed, as Lot was with conditions in Sodom. While devout Pre-millennialists are compelled to recognize these sad facts, they, at the same time, rejoice that it is the dark hour before the dawn of the coming "day of our Lord." They hold steadfastly to their faith, labor with holy zeal to rescue the perishing, and lift up their hearts with gratitude and praise as they see prophecy fulfilled, and believe with all their hearts, that "the coming of the Lord draweth nigh."

CHAPTER X.

THE MILLENNIUM.

In the preceding chapter we had something to say of the great apostasy foretold as coming into the church as we approach the end of the present age. Much more could have been said on this subject; we might call attention to the fact that Spain, Italy, France, Mexico, and South America are under the fearful blight of the apostate Roman Church; all these countries, where practically all of the inhabitants have received what is supposed to be Christian baptism, have so fearfully apostatized from the Christian faith that they have become most needy mission fields.

If possible, the Greek Catholic Church is still more apostate, and has so completely fallen away from the true spirit of Christianity that the Russian people are in revolt against the Christian religion; and all those countries that have been under the influence of the Greek Church are needy fields for missionary activity and the preaching of a saving gospel. So far as genuine spiritual life is concerned, or any sort of true evangelism to bring repentance and saving faith to the people, one could hardly imagine a more apostate condition of things than exists in those countries dominated by the Roman and Greek churches.

Germany is under the blight of destructive criticism, which has not only gone forward in the destruction of any spiritual life, but has sent her influence abroad destroying the faith to a fearful extent in Protestant countries. England and the United States, where Protestantism has had the best opportunities, and wielded a powerful influence for good, have felt, in a startling degree, the spiritual paralysis that has come over from Germany. Just now the church of the United States is passing through a period of unbelief that is startling to contemplate. There are but a few theological seminaries left among the Protestant nations that are not largely dominated by men who have been so influenced by German destructive criticism that they have almost entirely given up evangelical faith. The dangerous and Christ-dishonoring spirit is abroad in the land. Scores and hundreds of young ministers are going out from these seminaries to disseminate teachings entirely out of harmony with the teachings of our Lord and His disciples.

The public press of this nation is friend-

ly to the theory of evolution and modern liberalism, and quite inclined to hold up to con-
tempt and ridicule orthodox Christian faith,
and all those who adhere strictly to the divine inspiration and authority of the Bible,
and a pure gospel, which is the power of
God unto salvation.

All of this produces an atmosphere antagonistic to spiritual life, to a pure, dogmatic gospel, to revivals of religion, where
sinners are soundly saved and brought to
Christ. It takes the supernatural, the
spirit and power out of our Christianity; in
fact, it turns Christianity, with the sinful-
ness of mankind, the blood atonement of
Christ, and the regeneration of the individual by the power of the Holy Ghost, into a
mere religion, a system of education, of programs, duties, entertainments; it humanizes
the whole realm of religion and makes salvation, if there is any need left for such
thing, to depend upon a man's culture and
his own works, rather than upon faith in an
atoning Christ.

Recently there has been organized in
the City of New York, an association of infidels; this association has been granted a
certificate of incorporation by the State of
New York. Mr. Charles Smith, the president of this blasphemous organization, tells

us that, "There are in this country millions of atheists, whom agitation will precipitate into militancy and who, when united, can overthrow the religious terrorism that frustrates their pursuits of happiness."

He goes on to say "Our association will endeavor to stop religion in public schools, prevent the issuance of religious proclamations by government officials, and to erase the inscriptions on coins. Our main purpose will be to wage war on religion. Christianity must give way to humanism, which will exalt above all things, the beauty and power of man. Meetings will be held in this city. Local branches are being formed in practically every state. National lecturers will be placed in the field. Representatives will be sent abroad. One such representative can undo the work of scores of missionaries, and a few thousand dollars will more than offset as many millions spent by the churches. Cheap editions of the works of the great free thinkers will be be published and placed within the reach of everybody. We believe that religion has had a fair chance to prove its metal, but it has proved altogether inadequate."

Here you have a bold declaration of war against God, His Church, and the Christianity of this nation. One of the most inter-

esting features of this situation is the fact
that this declaration seems to have made
no serious impression upon the Church.
Why is this? Perhaps, the religious sensi-
tiveness of the Christian public has been
destroyed by its hero worship of one of its
great pulpit idols, who has openly denied the
virgin birth of the Lord Jesus, or that He
ever wrought any miracles, or that there
is any special need of a blood atonement;
with these, of course, goes the denial of the
bodily resurrection of Christ. And now, to
this great apostle of modern liberalism,
millionaires of New York who claim to be
Christians, are to build a temple costing
some four millions of dollars from whose
pulpit he is to attack the deity of Jesus
Christ.

Bold and blasphemous as is this atheis-
tic society, it will not do anything approaching the harm that will be brought about by
skeptical teaching in our church schools, and
religious literature which proposes to sub-
stitute repentance and faith with the regenerating power of the Holy Ghost, by teaching the Catechism and persuading children,
on some set day, to make a "decision." These
atheists are emboldened by the skepticism
springing up in the church, everywhere, denying and setting aside the supernatural

power of God, as revealed in His word, and experienced by the individual in the regenerating and sanctifying power of the Holy Ghost.

It is the paralysis which has been brought into the Methodist, Baptist, and Presbyterian churches, the three great Protestant bodies of this nation, by the teachings of the destructive critics and modern liberalists, that provides a way, and the conditions for the organization and work of these blasphemous societies in the nation and universities, that proposes to defy God, destroy the Bible, and overthrow the Christian Church.

We do not overlook the fact that there are many devout people and faithful preachers in the world. We rejoice in the fact that there is much evangelical Christianity in this nation; a very large percent, however, of these evangelical Christians who are untainted by modernism and are standing faithfully for the word of God, and His supernatural power in the salvation of men, are Pre-millennialists, and these Pre-millennialists are full of faith and hope for the future of the race. They believe that we are rapidly approaching the overthrow of Satan and his power, the coming of our Lord, and the bringing in of a reign of peace

on earth. This holy optimism stimulates
their activities in seeking to spread the gospel, promote revivals, and bring every soul,
possible, to repentance and saving faith;
and notwithstanding the apostasy of the
times, the distress of nations, and the dark-
ness of the day, they are singing with joy in
their hearts, at the thought that the dark-
ness soon will have passed, and the Sun of
righteousness shall arise with healing in
His beams.

CONDITIONS DURING THE MILLENNIUM.

Quite naturally, the question arises,
What sort of a world shall we have when
Jesus comes?   This is a legitimate and interesting question.   The only light we have
on the subject is what is taught and sug-
gested by the Holy Scriptures.

First of all, it is to be a warless age. The
word of God plainly declares that "men
shall learn war no more."   Think what a
change this will bring into human history!
The history of the race has been one of war,
bloodshed, destruction of life and property,
followed by disease and plague. Thank God,
the time is coming when wars shall cease
and peace shall reign on earth. We are told
that ninety-five percent of the taxes of this
great nation is used for purposes of war;
the building of battleships, airships, the

training and support of military organizations. All highly civilized, so-called Christian nations, carry a crushing burden of taxes for the same purpose. It would be impossible to enumerate the untold millions of money that is spent in a quarter of a century in the organization, support of armies, building of navies, and carrying on the bloody strife among human beings. The most highly civilized nations of the world have just been compelled to bow their heads, and take upon their necks, the iron yoke of a taxation slavery that they must carry for sixty years. Think of it! Two generations of people yet unborn must stagger under the burden of taxes to be gathered to pay for the slaughter of ten millions of young men slain in the World War.

Take all of your expert historians and lightning calculators, and put them to work to enumerate the money spent, the lives lost, the property destroyed, the blood spilt, the tears shed, and the wreck and ruin that have come to humanity in the past thousand years because of war, and then think of a thousand years without war! The optimistic Pre-millennialists who are constantly accused of being pessimists, believe that we are rapidly approaching a period when the Lord Jesus will appear, overthrow wickedness, bring in a reign of peace and happiness among men which shall last for a thousand years. This is the highest and most optimistic outlook that human beings can possibly contemplate.

God grant us a thousand years in which the money used for the past thousand years for war, shall be used for the building of comfortable, sanitary homes, the construction of good highways everywhere; the building of dams to supply water power that will bring to the people by the pressing of a button, all the light, heat, and power that will be necessary for their comfort and the carrying on of industries that will contribute to the welfare and happiness of humanity.

Think of the hospitals that can be built for the care of the sick, of the research that can easily be set on foot for the scientific discovery of the cause and preventing of disease; of the great plants that can be erected for the production of cheap and excellent fertilizer; of the drainage system that can bring into cultivation untold millions of acres of fertile swamp land; of the barriers that can be erected to prevent the overflow of streams; of the homes that can be built for the care and comfort of the old and infirm; of the care and protection that can be offered for the preservation of the health and life of babes; of the bounties that will be yielded by the fields of cereals, vegetables and fruits; of the invention of farming utensils that will relieve the hardships of labor, of the disappearance, most altogether, of mules and horses, which have been the hard-worked servants of mankind, and necessarily consumed such a large percent of the productions of the earth; of the development of the highest grades of milch cows, that will supply an abundance of healthful nourishment for the growing generations that shall populate the new earth. Think of spiritual and social conditions, when immoral diseases will have disappeared, and inherited tendencies that weaken body and mind, shall be almost unknown.

Think of a period in the history of humanity when, instead of a spirit of avarice, covetousness and strife, men shall co-operate with each other in beautiful harmony in supplying the needs of humanity and, instead of spiteful competition, there shall be brotherly love and helpfulness in the realm of business enterprise. Think of a world without a distillery of intoxicants, a saloon, or a drunken man! Think of a time when you will not need to put locks on your doors, or cash registers in your places of business, or have federal prisons for the incarceration of trusted bankers who have squandered the money of the people. Think of a period of history when London will have no slums, Paris no palaces of prostitution, Chicago no corrupt police force, or robbers roaming the streets, with rapid-fire guns; when New York, with its vast population of mixed multitudes from all nations, will come to realize and rejoice in a consciousness of the fatherhood of God and the brotherhood of men, through the redeeming power of Christ.

The ancient prophet saw this Golden Age and tried to give us some conception of it. Micah says: "But in the last days it shall come to pass, that the mountain of the house of the Lord will be established in the top of the mountains, and it shall be exalted above the hills; and people shall flow into it. And many nations shall come, and say, Come, and let us go up to the mountain of the Lord, unto the house of the God of Jacob; and he will teach us his ways, and we will walk in his paths: For the law shall go forth of Zion, and the word of the Lord from Jerusalem. And he shall judge among the people, and rebuke strong nations afar off; and they shall beat their swords into plowshares, and their spears into pruninghooks:

Nation shall not lift up sword against nation, neither shall they learn war any more. But they shall sit every man under his vine and fig tree, and none shall make them afraid: For the mouth of the Lord of hosts hath spoken it." Micah 4:1-4.

With what optimistic joy we of the Premillennial faith look forward to these glorious days of the Kingdom of God upon earth. The world will be evangelized rapidly; men will still be free agents; the individual must choose and be saved by faith in Christ, but Satan overthrown, Jesus reigning in His glory, doubt will be difficult, faith will be easy. Africa will be evangelized. Roads, like streets, will cross her vast forests and plains, her people will be civilized, clothed and dwell in comfortable homes. Educated and illumined by the Spirit, they will, perhaps, be the greatest singers in all the world. Wireless communication will have been so perfectly developed that the Lord of lords and King of kings can sit upon the throne of universal empire in Jerusalem, and speak the same message to every human being on the globe.

Words fail us! The prophet could not find speech to express the glory of the vision which stretched before him, and he cried out, "The earth shall be full of the knowledge of the Lord, as the waters cover the sea." The joy of the people is expressed by Isaiah, when he says, "And in that day they shall say, Praise the Lord, call upon his name, declare his doings among the people, make mention that his name is exalted. Sing unto the Lord; for he hath done excellent things: This is known in all the earth. Cry out and shout, thou inhabitant of Zion: For great is the Holy One of Israel in the midst of thee!" Isa. 12:4-6.

CHAPTER XI.

JESUS IS COMING BACK TO THIS EARTH.

The bodily return of our Lord Jesus Christ to this earth is so plainly and repeatedly taught by the Lord Himself and His apostles, that there can be no question about His coming in the minds of all Christian people who fully accept the divine inspiration of the Scriptures. Whether we be pre or post-millennial in our views, we believe that the Lord Jesus will return. The Lord Himself said before the high priest and His accusers, "Hereafter shall ye see the Son of man sitting on the right hand of power, and coming in the clouds of heaven." When He ascended, bodily, into the heavens, and His disciples "looked steadfastly toward heaven as he went up, behold, two men stood by them in white apparel; which also said, Ye men of Galilee, why stand ye gazing up into heaven? This same Jesus, which is taken up from you into heaven, shall so come in like manner as ye have seen him go into heaven." Acts 1:11.

We could quote many other scriptures that tell us as plainly as inspired men could write, that the Lord Jesus will return visibly, to this world. It was one of the last promises that He made to His followers, and through them to all of His followers, in all time. For some three centuries the coming of the Lord was the hope and inspiration of the church. Whatever their persecutions and sufferings, they were constantly comforted with the thought that Jesus Christ would come in glory and power, that He would overthrow the unjust and cruel reign of wicked men and establish a reign of peace and righteousness.

Saint Peter gives great comfort to persecuted believers, and believers of all time, when he said: "Nevertheless we, according to his promise, look for new heavens and new earth, wherein dwelleth righteousness. Wherefore, beloved, seeing that ye look for such things, be diligent that ye may be found of him in peace, without spot, and blameless." 2 Pet. 3:13, 14.

Our Post-millennial friends with pessimistic outlook, put far away into the future, perhaps ten, fifty, or a hundred thousand years, the coming of the Lord, and make the unscriptural claim that, before His coming, the entire world will be brought to repentance and saving faith, by the preaching of the gospel. This view, entirely out of harmony with the Scriptures, robs

each successive generation for an almost un-
limited period of time to come, of all possibility of hope of His coming, and takes away
the stimulus for service, the joy and comfort in time of trouble that come to Christian hearts that nurse the "blessed hope" of
the appearing of the Lord.

Of what value is the exhortation of the
Lord Jesus that we "Watch", that we keep
our lamps trimmed and burning, with oil
in our vessels, if we are fully convinced that
there is no sort of possibility of His coming
for untold thousands of years. The teaching that the population of the earth will be
saved by the preaching of the gospel before
the coming of the Lord, is out of harmony
with the teaching of the Lord on the subject. Jesus teaches us that many will be
unprepared when He shall appear in His
glory, and that these unprepared ones will
call for the rocks and mountains to fall
upon, and cover them. No doubt the appearance of the Lord will be embarrassing,
fearful indeed, to those brilliant and popular preachers who are denying His virgin
birth, Godhead, blood atonement, bodily resurrection, and second coming.

The Lord teaches us that His appearance will be as sudden and unexpected as
was the flood in the days of Noah. They

were "eating and drinking, marrying and giving in marriage, until the day that Noah entered into the ark, and knew not until the flood came, and took them all away; so shall also the coming of the Son of man be. Then shall two be in the field; the one shall be taken, and the other left. Two women shall be grinding at the mill; the one shall be taken, and the other left. Watch ye therefore: for ye know not what hour your Lord doth come." Matt. 24:37-42.

In this same lesson the Lord shows us very clearly that all men will not be prepared when He comes. He speaks of certain evil servants who shall say in their hearts, "My Lord delayeth his coming; and shall begin to smite his fellow-servants, and to eat and drink with the drunken; the Lord of that servant shall come in a day when he looketh not for him, and in an hour that he is not aware of, and shall cut him asunder, and appoint him his portion with the hypocrites: There shall be weeping and gnashing of teeth." Matt. 24:48-51.

It would be easy to add many passages of scripture of like character to these just quoted, but it is unnecessary. We will call attention to the fact that the parable of the wise and foolish virgins is a very clear setting forth of the fact that a large percent of professed Christians, when our Lord shall appear, will be only Christians in appearance; with the outside form of religion, but entirely lacking in spirit, without the Holy Ghost in their hearts.

There is nothing contained in the teaching of Christ or His disciples, upon which to base the belief that at any time before the second coming of our Lord, the entire human race will be brought into fellowship with Him, and His Kingdom, in any true sense, set up on earth. Exactly the reverse of this is taught. Our Lord Jesus in all of His teachings points to a future of rebellion against God, of unbelief, of rejection of His gospel message of salvation, of the persecution of His disciples, and encourages His faithful followers to fortitude and patience in view of the fact that He will return to them.

The program of God provides, in Jesus Christ, salvation for all men. The gospel must be preached in all the world, mercy proclaimed and warning given. Those who repent and believe in the Lord Jesus shall be saved, and those who refuse to repent and reject Him, will be lost. There is no coercion in the plan of salvation. God works along the line of revelation; He strives to enlighten men, to teach them the great facts of their origin, their duty, and their destiny, and everywhere, gives them to understand that their salvation depends upon their own choice; abundant provisions for their redemption are made. "Whosoever will, may come." But those who refuse to come must perish.

There is nothing more trivial and out of harmony with the facts than the accusation which is frequently brought against Premillennialists, that according to their theory of teaching, that God having failed with the gospel plan of setting up His Kingdom in the world, must needs have recourse to force and come with arbitrary power, setting up His Kingdom and compelling men, against their own wills, to become His obedient subjects. We fear that the teaching of some Pre-millennialists afford some ground for accusations of this character. It is unfortunate that any Pre-millennialist teacher should have given occasion and opportunity for any such accusation.

The long period of years stretching between the first and second coming of our Lord Jesus has been a period of gracious probation and gospel grace; a time for the evangelization of the world, the sanctification of the church. Christ by the grace of God, tasted death for every man; and the command of Jesus was to go into all the world and preach the gospel to every creature. No man has any right to place any sort of limit upon the atonement made by Christ, or the gracious offers made in the gospel. There is no hint from Jesus or any of the inspired writers, that all of the people in any community, of any generation, or any period in the history of the race, prior to His second coming, will receive the gospel. We are taught always, and everywhere, that there are those who reject and oppose the Lord Jesus and His message of mercy.

We most firmly believe that post-millennial teaching is very largely responsible for the fact that the gospel has not been preached in all the world. Post-millennialic have put far away the coming of the Lord. They have not made haste to carry the message of God's love, and salvation in Jesus, to the lost multitudes in heathen lands. Losing sight of the fact that Jesus is to return, suddenly, and unexpectedly, to set up a kingdom of peace and good will among men, they have built up great ecclesiasticisms, wasted untold millions of money in vast cathedrals, and in palaces for the rulers in the churches; and these ecclesiastical organizations have gone to war with each other, and while untold millions have died without the gospel, they have been living in strife and fierce competition to see who could enroll the most members, build the highest steeples, collect the largest sums of money, and drift farthest away from the plain teachings of the Holy Scriptures, and adjust themselves more nearly to the world's fashions and customs, that they might increase their number of adherents and larger collections in their coffers.

At this very hour, when missionary work is being curtailed, missionaries are being called home from the field, schools for the education of the children of heathen parents are being dismissed for lack of funds, vast church buildings are being erected all over this nation, costing hundreds of thousands of dollars, and even millions, to foster ecclesiastical ambition and pride, while the poor heathen die without the knowledge that God so loved the world, that He gave His only begotten Son for its redemption. This is a misdirected program, in harmony with the spirit of Post-millennialism that puts so far away the glorious appearing of our Lord, that it has ample time to foster these follies while millions remain who have never heard the gospel. Meanwhile, there is being cultivated a spirit of bitterness and resentment against those who rejoice in the blessed hope of the soon appearing of our Lord, which amounts to persecution. Men, high in authority, in Methodism, have been instructed to reject any young minister knocking at the doors of an annual conference, for admission, if he is pre-millennial in his views with reference to the second coming of Christ. Such an official is an ecclesiastical tyrant, and bitter persecutor of his Lord, and the faith and teachings of the inspired apostles.

It should not be forgotten that, while a fearful extravagance characterizes the home program of Post-millennialists, that missionaries are being fostered in the foreign field, and sent out from the homeland, who are fearfully modernistic and liberal in their attitude toward the Bible and our Lord Jesus. It is claimed, with the appearance of truth, that most all of our theological seminaries which are dominated by the post-millennial spirit, are unsound in their teachings, and are sending forth a young ministry so tainted with modern destructive criticism, that they will promote unbelief, rather than an evangelical experience, which will promote revivals of religion, and bring about the salvation of the lost multitudes.

Had the church held on to its original pre-millennial teaching, and looked with joy to the glorious appearing of her Saviour and Lord, she would have remembered His command to carry the gospel to every creature; she would have remembered that He said, "When this gospel of the kingdom shall be preached in all the world for a witness to all nations; and then shall the end come," and would have hastened with the glad news of God's love and Christ's redeeming power.

Faithfulness to the pre-millennial teaching would have made Roman Catholicism an impossibility. Had the church held faithfully to her original views and teaching on the second coming of Christ, millions of money could never have been piled up in the vast cathedrals, palaces, monuments, marble images, magnificent robes, and bejeweled crowns, with popes, cardinals, and bishops, absorbing untold millions in palaces and great salaries; but simplicity of life would have prevailed, comfortable tabernacles would have been erected, and these millions wasted upon ecclesiastical pride would have gone for the world's evangelization.

Had the Roman Church built no cathedrals and lifted up to high officialism certain men, Protestantism would not have followed her bad example in the same pride and wastefulness, in fact, there would have been no need for Protestantism. Pre-millennial teaching and views constantly kept before the people, they would have been faithful to the inspiration of the Scriptures, the deity of our Lord and the tremendous importance of bringing the gospel speedily to every creature.

Suppose the church had held on to the pre-millennial coming of Christ, as she did for the first centuries of her rapid spread and holy devotion! Suppose the entire Christian world had been thoroughly permeated with the belief and hope that the Lord Jesus is to appear in glory with His saints and angels, to set up a kingdom of righteousness and peace on earth! How impossible the last World War would have been, and all the terrible wars of the last century. The crowned heads of the world, claimed to be baptized believers, have been powerfully influenced by the Christian doctrines they have been taught. Suppose the Kaiser of Germany had been an ardent Pre-millennialist, the Czar of Russia, King of Italy, of Great Britain, of Belgium, the President and Premier of France, the King of Austria, and other heads of the European nations engaged in this fearful slaughter,

had have been faithful believers in the pre-
millennial coming of our Lord, how impossible the World War! How utterly impossible the conditions that brought on this
slaughter of men! They were all professed
Christians, church members, but they were
post-millennial in their views; none of them
desired the coming of the Lord, none of them
expected His appearing for millenniums yet
to come, if at all; they had their own programs, and ignored the fact that God had
any program, and behold, the slaughter of
millions, the starvation of multitudes of human beings, the plague following that swept
its countless millions of helpless human beings into their graves before they had lived
out half their days!

Pre-millennialists are the most optimistic people in all the world. They have a
faith that stimulates them to glad and earnest service and joyful anticipation. They
are holding steadfastly to the inspiration of
the Scriptures, the virgin birth, the deity,
blood atonement, bodily resurrection, and
the glorious second coming of the Lord Jesus. They believe with happy hearts and
joyful songs, that the "kingdoms of this
world are to become the kingdoms of our
Lord and his Christ." That heaven and
earth may unite in the glad chorus of the

angels that startled the shepherds who watched their flocks on Judean hills when Christ was born in Bethlehem: "Glory to God in the highest! Peace on earth, good will to men."

www.ingramcontent.com/pod-product-compliance
Lightning Source LLC
Chambersburg PA
CBHW021154020426
42331CB00003B/47